A Family Money-Go-Round Special

A Consumer's Guide to Leaving Money to Children

A Family Money-Go-Round
Special

A Consumer's Guide to Leaving Money to Children

John Turner

Series editor
Richard Northedge

Published by the
Daily Telegraph
in association with Woodhead-Faulkner

Published by the Daily Telegraph
135 Fleet Street, London EC4P 4BL

First published 1984
© Daily Telegraph 1984
ISBN 0 86367 033 4

British Library Cataloguing in Publication Data
Turner, John
    A consumer's guide to leaving money to children. – (A Family Money-go-Round Special.)
    1. Inheritance and transfer tax – Law and legislation – Great Britain. 2. Tax planning – Great Britain.
    I. Title. II. Series.
    344.103513   KD5560
    ISBN 0 86367 033 4.

Text design by Geoff Green
Typeset by Hands Fotoset, Leicester
Printed in Great Britain by St Edmundsbury Press, Bury St Edmunds, Suffolk

Author's preface

Most of us acquire a modest amount of money and possessions during our working lives: a house, some savings, the odd assurance policy and perhaps a valuable or two. When we die, we want our families to enjoy the benefit of these things; we certainly wish to minimise the amount of tax that the Inland Revenue extracts from what we leave.

This concern is not one only for the very wealthy; savings and possessions worth £100,000 – not excessive when the value of a typical house is taken into account – could produce a capital transfer tax liability on death of over £11,500. Yet in practice, there is considerable scope for legally reducing capital transfer tax liabilities. With suitable planning, a married couple could pass on almost half a million pounds to their children without paying a penny piece in capital transfer tax; it is much simpler for less wealthy mortals to pass on smaller amounts free of tax.

This book outlines the tax rules covering passing money on and explains the reliefs and exemptions which enable those who plan ahead to maximise the amount that goes to their family. In the longer term, most people aim to pass money on to their children and grandchildren, but this book also explains how to provide for a husband or wife and, perhaps, ageing relatives or friends. It also deals with gifts and bequests to charities and other good causes, for which there are considerable tax incentives. Incidentally, the term 'child' is used throughout this book to mean adult children as well as minors unless it is specifically stated otherwise and it is assumed that both husband and wife are domiciled in the UK.

There is not sufficient space in a book of this sort to cover all the eccentricities of the UK tax system, and therefore it should not be treated as anything more than a general introduction. No action should be taken without discussing your particular set of circumstances with professional advisers.

I have incorporated relevant changes in the tax legislation up to and including the Finance Act of 1984.

Many colleagues in Peat Marwick's Norwich and London offices have contributed to this book with help and advice and their assistance has been invaluable. I thank them all, and acknowledge that any errors and omissions are entirely my own responsibility.

September 1984   John Turner

Contents

Chapter 1

Estate planning

Your estate is usually understood to be what you leave when you die; throughout this book, the term will apply to your wealth and possessions in life or death. Estate planning will describe what can be done to ensure that the maximum amount of what you own passes to your heirs.

The first step in considering estate planning is to work out what you are worth now – then, once the scale of the problem is known, you can begin to seek solutions.

How much are you worth?

Table 1 will help you to work out the value of your estate if you were to die tomorrow. If you are married, fill in one column for yourself, one for your husband or wife. If either of the totals exceeds £64,000, then alarm bells should ring – if you or your spouse died tomorrow, there could be a capital transfer tax liability. If the totals are below this limit but you have been giving substantial amounts away in the past ten years, the same could apply. And if your joint total exceeds £64,000, you should also give some thought to estate planning – if one of you dies leaving everything to the other, the survivor's estate could be large enough to incur capital transfer tax.

Even if none of these applies to you now, it is worth peering into the future. In a few years' time, your mortgage may be paid off, or you might receive a lump sum on retirement, for example; either could boost your estate into the danger zone.

13

Table 1: How much are you worth?

Assets	Husband £	Wife £
Home and other property: market value less outstanding mortgages		
Money in the bank		
building society		
National Savings		
other deposits		
Investments – stocks, shares and unit trusts		
Life assurance – amount paid out on death (including any bonuses)		
Valuables – antiques, jewellery, etc.		
Car(s)		
Other possessions – furniture, dinghy, etc.		
Loans – money you are owed		
Business/farm – value		
Interests in trusts, wills or settlements		
LESS outstanding loans (except mortgages which are included in Home and other property)		
TOTAL		

Writing a will

If you have not yet drawn up a will, or your will was drawn up some time ago, it is essential to consider what you want to happen to your estate on death. A will may be re-arranged after your death (as may a distribution according to the laws of intestacy if you die without a will). However, it is a lot less complicated and considerably cheaper to leave a properly considered will, and the subject of wills is covered in greater depth in Chapter 14.

Drawing up a will also begins to sharpen up the issues that must be faced in estate planning. At one extreme, it may remove the need for estate planning altogether: a single person without dependants may wish to give a lot of money to charity – these gifts are free of tax even if your estate is over £64,000. At the other extreme, a young parent will probably want everything to go to a surviving spouse (also tax-free) or for the benefit of the children if both should die (irrespective of the tax consequences).

For most people, however, it will begin to raise questions such as:

- Should I leave everything to my husband or wife, or something to others?
- What should a surviving spouse aim to do with the money?
- Do I want to pass on a family business or farm to my heirs?
- Will my children wish to live in my house (so that I should take steps to make sure they do not have to sell it to pay tax), or will they sell it anyway?

An estate planning programme

To make estate planning easier, it is sensible to draw up a list of priorities. For example, if passing on a family business or house is a prime consideration, then the steps to ensure this should form the centrepiece of your estate planning strategy: other gifts should be planned once the prime objectives are secured, and funds held in reserve to pay any tax liabilities which might threaten the plans.

An essential part of estate planning is to consider your own needs in later years, and those of your husband or wife. It is all too easy to devise a plan to cheat the taxman which leaves the planner to a miserable and penurious retirement; counting on the charity of other members of the family is a recipe for family strife. A pension scheme is usually the most tax-efficient way of providing for old age and can also offer benefits to your spouse after your death without tax complications (the self-employed can obtain similar benefits with a retirement annuity).

Once you have drawn up your programme, it must be regularly reviewed (in conjunction with your will). Your circumstances will change, as will those of the people you hope to benefit by your planning. Tax laws will change – it is only just over ten years since capital transfer tax was introduced; many of the exemptions in this book were introduced in the years since. Apart from major changes in the legislation, many thresholds and exemptions increase from time to time, and planning should take account of that. And particular circumstances may make a gift opportune which would otherwise incur excessive tax – a temporary fall in share prices can allow a major gift of securities at reduced tax cost, for example.

Life assurance

Paying the premiums on life assurance policies is often a good way of passing on money (see Chapter 4). But life assurance also has a part to play in ensuring that unforeseen events do not spoil your plans.

For example, as pointed out in Chapter 2, extra capital transfer tax may be due if you die within three years of making a gift. *Term life assurance* can be arranged to pay out enough money to cover the tax liability if you die within that three-year period, so that the recipient will not have to find the extra tax.

Another type of planning outlined in Chapter 4 suggests making large gifts at ten-year intervals. If you are passing on a large asset such as a home or business in instalments at ten-year intervals, an untimely death could mean tax to pay on whatever has not yet been handed over – perhaps forcing your heirs to sell some of what you had hoped to pass on to them intact. *Term life assurance* could cover for this eventuality by paying out if you died before the whole asset has been transferred.

And if you know that there will be a tax liability when you die and can see no way of avoiding it, *whole life assurance* (which pays out whenever you die) may be the answer.

Using this book

The rest of this book is in two parts: Chapters 2 and 3 outline the basic tax framework of estate planning; the remainder looks at how that framework applies to passing on particular types of asset – cash, valuables, houses, businesses and so on.

Sadly, this book cannot tell you exactly what to do; that depends on your specific circumstances, and the solution will be different for every reader. What the book will tell you is how the taxes will apply to the things you own, and ways of reducing the liability. In some cases, you will face difficult choices: it may not be possible to pass on both business and house in a short period of time, for example. Or passing on one of these objects may make it harder to pass on other possessions.

It may also be that reading this book shows you the need for professional advice. If your affairs are at all complicated, your estate is large or there is a business to be passed on, a chartered accountant can advise. The services of a solicitor may also be essential in dealing with legal aspects of estate planning, especially the will. Armed with the knowledge gleaned from these pages, you will be better able to explain the problems you face to your professional advisers – and understand their solutions. Beware, however, of those who offer advice on estate planning as a way of selling their investment products; all the options must be considered in drawing up a plan, and not just the products of a particular firm or sector.

Above all, once you have sorted out the size of the problem you face, you can begin to plan out your strategy. And as the book shows, while you might not be able to pass everything on, lock, stock and barrel, there is considerable scope for making sure that the fruits of your labour are enjoyed by your heirs.

Chapter 2

Capital transfer tax

Capital transfer tax is the main tax which people are seeking to avoid by estate planning. It was introduced in 1974 to replace estate duty and, like that tax, is payable on the value of what you leave on death. However, unlike estate duty, it is also payable on gifts made throughout your lifetime – though there are considerable concessions which allow tax-free gifts to be made. It may also be payable on gifts made by a person outside the UK who counts as 'domiciled' in the UK (for example, an expatriate or recent emigrant – see Appendix C).

This chapter looks at capital transfer tax, and how the tax is assessed. Later chapters look in more detail at how capital transfer tax is applied in specific instances, such as to gifts of money, shares, valuables, land and so on.

The basis of capital transfer tax

The basic principle of capital transfer tax is that you pay tax if your estate (i.e. what you own) is reduced because of a *transfer of value*. Gifts and all property passed on at death count as transfers of value, and so, in certain circumstances, can a sale of an asset at less than market value.

Some transfers of value are exempt: for example, gifts between husband and wife, gifts in consideration of marriage (within limits) and certain other lifetime gifts. Up to £3,000 a year of gifts which are not exempt under these specific reliefs is also free of capital transfer tax – these exemptions are described more fully in Chapter 4.

Transfers of value which are not exempt are added to the total value of chargeable transfers made in the previous ten years to produce a cumulative total. The first slice of this cumulative total is taxed at the nil rate of capital transfer tax (the first £64,000 in 1984/85). Anything over the upper limit of the nil rate band is taxed at progressive rates.

On death, there is a 'deemed transfer of value' – i.e. everything left (your estate) is assumed to be given away as a single gift. The capital transfer tax liability is calculated by adding the taxable value of the estate to the cumulative total of taxable gifts made in the previous ten years, and taxing this at double the rates for lifetime gifts. This higher tax scale is also applied retrospectively to gifts made in the three years before death, so that death-bed gifts cannot be used to avoid the heavier rate for legacies.

Table 2 sets out the rates of capital transfer tax for the 1984/85 tax year – the thresholds for the various bands normally increase each year in line with inflation. When calculating the tax liability on a gift, it is the rates in force at the time of the gift which apply: if rates subsequently fall, there is no adjustment to the tax liabilities already assessed; equally, any further gifts are taxed at the new rates, even if a higher liability would have been due under the old rates.

Table 2: Capital transfer tax rates for 1984/85

Cumulative total of gifts in previous 10 years	Lifetime gifts		Gifts on death, or within 3 years of death	
	Rate	Cumulative tax	Rate	Cumulative tax
£	%	£	%	£
0–64,000	0	–	0	–
64,001–85,000	15	3,150	30	6,300
85,001–116,000	17.5	8,575	35	17,150
116,001–148,000	20	14,975	40	29,950
148,001–185,000	22.5	23,300	45	46,600
185,001–232,000	25	35,050	50	70,100
232,001–285,000	27.5	49,625	55	99,250
285,001 or over	30	–	60	–

Who pays the tax?

With gifts during lifetime, either the giver or the recipient can pay the capital transfer tax. With gifts of certain assets such as houses and businesses, if the recipient pays the tax, it can be paid in instalments over ten years.

For gifts on death, the tax is generally paid out of the estate; if there are a number of specific bequests to people such as children and grandchildren, the tax is paid out of what is left (the residue) unless the giver directs that a bequest is to suffer its own share of tax. Again, with certain bequests such as houses or businesses, the tax may be paid in instalments.

If the giver dies within three years of making a gift, extra capital transfer tax may be due since the gift is taxed at the higher rates applicable on death – in this case, the recipient pays the extra tax irrespective of who paid in the first place.

Grossing-up

If the giver pays the tax on a gift, the amount paid counts as part of the transfer of value. This principle causes no problems if tax is taken into account in making a gift: for example, if you wished to give away £100,000 to a child, then the tax on that gift would be £5,775 and the after-tax value of the gift £100,000 less £5,775 = £94,225. However, it is more usual to make the gift and then worry about the tax – i.e. to hand over the £100,000 and write another cheque for the tax. To have £100,000 after tax, a gift of £107,000 is required on which tax of £7,000 is due.

The process of adding the tax to the net (after-tax) gift to arrive at the size of the gross (before-tax) transfer of value is known as *grossing-up*. Table 3 allows you to calculate the grossed-up value for lifetime gifts for the 1984/85 rates of capital transfer tax.

Table 3:   Grossing-up of net lifetime transfers

Net transfers £	Tax payable £			£	Cumulative net transfers £	Totals gross equivalent £
0–64,000	Nil				64,000	64,000
64,001–81,850	Nil + 3/17	(17.647%) for each £ over	64,000	81,850	85,000
81,851–107,425	3,150 + 7/33	(21.212%)	,, ,, ,, ,,	81,850	107,425	116,000
107,426–133,025	8,575 + 1/4	(25%)	,, ,, ,, ,,	107,425	133,025	148,000
133,026–161,700	14,975 + 9/31	(29.032%)	,, ,, ,, ,,	133,025	161,700	185,000
161,701–196,950	23,300 + 1/3	(33.333%)	,, ,, ,, ,,	161,700	196,950	232,000
196,951–235,375	35,050 + 11/29	(37.931%)	,, ,, ,, ,,	196,950	235,375	285,000
235,376 or over	49,625 + 3/7	(42.875%)	,, ,, ,, ,,	235,375		

Example

John Smith gives £20,000 to his daughter on 10th May 1984, agreeing to pay any capital transfer tax due. The gift is taxable, and he has made taxable gifts in the previous ten years amounting to £70,000 (including tax).

The tax chargeable at current rates on the £70,000 of gifts already made comes to £900 (i.e. 15 per cent of the excess over £64,000 – see Table 2). Thus John Smith has given £70,000 – £900 = £69,100 of net gifts so far, and the latest net gift of £20,000 brings his total of net gifts to £89,100. He calculates the tax due on the new gift as follows:

Net transfers	Tax payable	£
£0–81,850	3/17 for each £ over £64,000	3,150
£81,851–86,100	7/33 for each £ over £81,850 (i.e. £4,250)	901
		4,051
Less: tax on previous transfers		900
Tax due on latest gift		3,151

Note that the tax due on the previous transfers is calculated at the current rates of capital transfer tax. If the £70,000 had been given before 13th March 1984, the tax paid would have been £1,500, not the £900 due under the 1984/85 rates; the difference between £1,500 and £900 is not refundable.

Valuation of property

The measure of a transfer of value is the amount by which the giver is out of pocket as a result of making the transfer. With most gifts, the starting point is the value of the gift itself – i.e. what it would fetch if sold on the open market.

However, with some gifts, the giver may be out of pocket by more than the value of the gift (even before grossing-up to allow for the tax paid). For example, if you give away shares which reduce your holding in a company from a controlling interest (i.e. over 50 per cent) to a minority one (i.e. under 50 per cent), then not only do you lose the value of the shares given away, you also lose the value of a controlling interest – and the chargeable transfer reflects this greater loss.

Likewise with collections, a gift which breaks up a set may reduce the value of the remaining incomplete set by more than the value of the individual item given away. For capital transfer tax purposes, it is the drop in value of your collection that is important in valuation, not the value of what is given away.

In calculating the value of your property, certain other 'related property' must be taken into account if this increases the value of your property. For example, if you own 30 per cent of the shares in a company and your wife owns 30 per cent, then the value of your shares is half the value of a 60 per cent holding (i.e. a controlling interest), rather than the value of a 30 per cent holding (i.e. a minority interest). Related property which must be taken into account in valuing a transfer is:

- that of a spouse;
- that given to charities, political parties or national institutions (see Chapter 13) in the past five years.

If property valued on death under these related property rules is sold within three years of the death at a loss compared to that value, the sale value may in certain circumstances be substituted for the related property value.

Associated operations

If a series of steps has a transfer of value as its end result, the Inland Revenue has the power to 'see through' the series of steps to discern the true nature of the operation. For example, if you give £64,000 to your spouse (a tax-free gift) on condition that he or she gives the money to someone else (perhaps to use the nil rate of capital transfer tax), then the gift made by the spouse will be treated as your gift – and taxed accordingly.

Under the rules against such associated operations, the Inland Revenue can treat as single transfers:

- any operations which affect the same property (for example, a house which passes along a chain of gifts);
- operations made which are conditional upon each other (for example, you give something to X on condition that X gives something to Y).

The associated operations provisions are complex and give the Inland Revenue wide powers to curb the use of tax avoidance schemes.

Mutual transfers

In certain circumstances, capital transfer tax on a gift can be repaid if the recipient makes a gift back to the giver. Such mutual transfers may occur if you give away some of your estate and later have to ask the recipient to give part of the gift back, or if a gift turns out to be liable to much more tax than expected (as can happen with unquoted shares – see Chapter 9).

Mutual transfer relief allows the gift back to be treated as an exempt transfer provided it is worth no more than the original gift. The original giver can also claim back the tax paid on the original gift (or on part of it if the gift back is worth less than the original gift). The gift back does not have to be the same property as the original gift to claim the relief. If the gift back is made more than 12 months after the original gift, the amount of the original gift cancelled is reduced by 4 per cent for each complete 12-month period between the two gifts.

With gifts of cash, calculating the amount of mutual transfer relief is relatively simple: if £100,000 is given, and £10,000 given back, the tax returned to the original giver is the difference between the tax due on a gift of £100,000 and that due on £90,000.

If the gift back is the same asset as was originally given, there may be capital transfer tax to pay if the asset has increased in value since the original gift was made (on the excess in value of the gift back over the original gift).

Relief for successive charges

If an estate left on death includes property received or inherited in the previous five years, the tax liability is reduced if capital transfer tax was paid on the property at the time it was received or inherited.

The amount of the reduction is a percentage of the tax already paid, depending on how long you have owned the property:
- 100 per cent if the property has been owned for less than one year;
- 80 per cent for property owned for between one and two years;

- 60 per cent for property owned for between two and three years;
- 40 per cent for property owned for between three and four years;
- 20 per cent for property owned for between four and five years.

Assessment and collection of capital transfer tax

Capital transfer tax – like most of the other taxes described in this book – is collected by the Inland Revenue. The tax operates on a self-assessment basis: there is no annual return, but the taxpayer is obliged to inform the Inland Revenue of any transfer of value which is not exempt from capital transfer tax if either of the following conditions are met:

- the amount of the gift plus any other chargeable transfers already made in the same tax year exceeds £10,000;
- the amount of the gift plus any other chargeable transfers already made in the previous ten years exceeds £40,000.

The transfer must be reported within 12 months of the end of the month in which the transfer of value takes place, or if later, within three months of the date that tax becomes due. Tax on lifetime transfers is normally due on 30th April in the following tax year or six months after the transfer, whichever is the later; for transfers on death, tax is due six months after the end of the month in which death occurs.

Interest is charged on late payment of tax – the rate is currently 6 per cent for transfers on death or 8 per cent in any other case. Since transfers may be reported up to three months after the date that tax becomes due, it is possible to face an interest charge for late payment of tax before there is a legal liability to make a return. As interest on late payment of tax does not qualify for income tax relief, consideration should be given to making a voluntary payment on account to avoid an interest charge.

The Inland Revenue office to tell is the Capital Taxes Office: for England and Wales, the address is Rockley Road, London W14 0DF; for Scotland, 16 Picardy Place, Edinburgh EH1 3NB; for Northern Ireland, Law Courts Building, Chichester Street, Belfast BT1 3NU.

Chapter 3

Other taxes

While capital transfer tax is the main target for estate planning, other taxes such as stamp duty, income tax and national insurance contributions all need to be borne in mind. However, perhaps the most important of the other taxes to be considered is capital gains tax: if gifts are made during a lifetime to save capital transfer tax, they may create a liability to capital gains tax which reduces or even eliminates the capital transfer tax savings. It is, therefore, capital gains tax with which this chapter begins.

Capital gains tax

Capital gains tax is a tax on gains made on lifetime disposals of a wide variety of assets – whether by sale or gift. The first slice of capital gains in a tax year is exempt from tax: for the 1984/85 tax year, the annual exemption limit is £5,600. Chargeable gains in excess of this figure are taxed at 30 per cent. This can be a serious liability in the case of a gift, where – in contrast to a sale – no cash is realised to pay the tax.

However, there are a number of important exemptions and reliefs which can reduce or even eliminate any liability to capital gains tax. For example, the disposal of your principal private home is free of capital gains tax, as are gifts of certain possessions. Many of these exemptions are dealt with later in this book under the chapter headings dealing with particular types of property.

25

Two important types of disposal exempt from capital gains tax are of particular interest when estate planning:

- *gifts between husband and wife* – provided the couple are both resident in the UK and are not separated. A couple who decide to split their possessions more equally between them (which can often make sense for minimising capital transfer tax) will pay no capital gains tax on the disposals involved;
- *disposals on death* – while all assets are assumed to have been disposed of on death, any gain is exempt from tax.

Assessment of capital gains tax

Capital gains tax is levied on the gain made on disposing of a chargeable asset – broadly the difference between its value at the time of acquisition and its value at the time of disposal. However, there are various allowances and deductions which can reduce the liability:

- *expenses* incurred in acquiring and disposing of the asset (for example, legal charges, improvement costs, valuations for sale and auctioneer's charges);
- *indexation allowance* which reflects increases in the Retail Price Index after the first 12 months of ownership (excluding any increase before March 1982);
- *losses* made on the disposal of other property in the same tax year or earlier tax years if not already used.

A fuller explanation of the rules for calculating capital gains tax liabilities is given in Appendix A.

Stamp duty

Certain types of gift can be made without the need for a legal process – money, stamp collections, jewellery, antiques and so on. However, other types of property can only change hands with the assistance of a legal document; stocks and shares and land and property are the most common examples. Stamp duty is payable on such documents and should be taken into account in planning gifts.

The rate of stamp duty is 1 per cent for transfers of stock and conveyances. Duty is not payable on transfers or conveyances of £30,000 or less, provided a certificate is given confirming the value and that the disposal is not part of an avoidance scheme;

once the £30,000 threshold is crossed, duty is payable on the whole amount.

There are special rules and rates for premiums on leases and for leases themselves.

Income tax

Income tax is a tax on all forms of income which fall within the following six schedules:

- Schedule A – income from property (e.g. rents);
- Schedule B – imputed income from the occupation of woodlands;
- Schedule C – income from government stock;
- Schedule D – subdivided into six cases, which cover profits from trades, professions and vocations, various types of investment income and income not covered by other schedules;
- Schedule E – income from employment (divided into three cases);
- Schedule F – dividends.

Income under all cases and schedules for the tax year is added together to produce *total income* (after certain payments known as outgoings are deducted – for example, interest on loans qualifying for tax relief, maintenance payments). After the taxpayer's personal allowances have been deducted, the balance – known as *taxable income* – is taxed at the *basic rate* (30 per cent for 1984/85), plus *higher rates* if in excess of a certain limit (£15,400 for 1984/85).

Taxation of wife's income

The income of a married woman living with her husband is treated as her husband's income for tax purposes: their income is aggregated and taxed as a single whole. The husband is entitled to claim the *married man's allowance* (£3,155 for 1984/85, compared with the *single person's allowance* of £2,005). If the wife has earnings of her own, *wife's earned income allowance* can be claimed in addition to the married man's allowance (£2,005 for 1984/85, or the amount of the wife's earnings if lower). There are special rules covering the tax year of marriage and when the marriage ends through divorce, separation or death.

If both husband and wife elect to do so, the wife's earnings can be taxed separately. Each is treated as a single person entitled to the single person's tax allowance for taxation of earnings (unearned income continues to be aggregated and assessed on the husband). In general, the wife's earnings election is worth while only if both husband and wife have reasonably high earnings, so that the amount of higher rate tax saved by separate taxation more than makes up for the loss of the higher married man's tax allowance.

Thus, whatever a husband and wife do, their investment income will be aggregated for income tax purposes. While it may make sense for a couple to share their possessions more equally to reduce capital transfer tax liabilities in the future, gifts of income-producing investments between spouses will not normally reduce their income tax liabilities.

Children

A minor – a child under the age of 18 – is treated as a separate individual for income tax purposes, entitled to his own personal tax allowance. However, income from gifts made by parents is taxed as if it was the parents' income.

Returns and claims may be made by a minor if married or in full-time employment; otherwise the parents have responsibility for these, and are liable for tax the child fails to pay.

If the child's total income is less than the single person's allowance (£2,005 for 1984/85), no tax is payable; investments where tax is deducted before interest is paid and cannot be refunded to a non-taxpayer should be avoided (for example building society and, in the future, bank deposit accounts).

National insurance contributions

National insurance contributions are effectively a tax on earned income which comes on top of income tax. The rates for the four classes of contributions in 1984/85 are given in Table 4.

While it may be advantageous to employ members of your family as part of estate planning, the possibility of national insurance contributions should always be borne in mind. For example, payments to an employee below the lower earnings limit are exempt from national insurance contributions; if just

Table 4: National insurance contributions 1984/85

Class 1 – Employees earning over £34 a week	Employee	Employer
Contracted in: on up to £250 a week of earnings	9.00%	10.45%
Contracted out: on first £34 a week of earnings	9.00%	10.45%
on next £216 a week of earnings	6.85%	6.35%

Class 2 – Self-employed	Flat-rate £4.60 per week if earnings over £1,850 a year

Class 3 – Voluntary	Flat-rate £4.50 per week

Class 4 – Self-employed	6.3% of profits between £3,950 and £13,000 a year

£1 over the lower earnings limit, contributions are payable on the whole amount by the employee at up to 9 per cent for 1984/85 (plus 10.45% by the employer). Thus, unless the payments are saving considerable amounts of tax elsewhere, it does not generally make sense to pay members of the family amounts just over the lower earnings limit.

Chapter 4

Gifts of money

The simplest way to pass property on is to give it away. Considerable amounts can be given away without paying capital transfer tax by taking advantage of the provisions for making tax-free gifts. This chapter looks at the amounts that can be given away in cash without paying tax; for gifts other than cash, there are capital gains tax complications which are dealt with in Chapter 6.

The following gifts can be made free of capital transfer tax:
- gifts to a husband or wife;
- gifts on marriage(within limits);
- gifts made out of 'normal income';
- 'small' gifts;
- gifts to support the giver's family;
- other gifts up to the value of the annual exemption limit each year (£3,000 in 1984/85);
- gifts in a ten-year period up to the upper limit of the nil rate tax band (up to £64,000 in 1984/85).

More details are given below.

With married couples, both husband and wife are entitled to these exemptions, and the limits described below are therefore effectively doubled for them.

Gifts to a spouse

Gifts to a husband or wife are exempt from capital transfer tax, provided both are domiciled in the United Kingdom, or are deemed to be domiciled in the United Kingdom (for more about domicile, see Appendix C). The exemption is removed if the marriage ends by divorce or annulment, but settlements made for the maintenance of the spouse or children at the time of the dissolution or under a court order are exempt.

The exemption on gifts between husband and wife can be extremely useful in avoiding capital transfer tax: if a married couple divide their wealth more equally between them, they will each be able to make tax free the other gifts outlined in this chapter, since a married couple is treated as two separate taxpayers for the purposes of capital transfer tax – each with their own allowances.

Gifts on marriage

Gifts made to a bride or groom on marriage are free of capital transfer tax within the following limits:
- £5,000 if the giver is a parent of the bride or groom;
- £2,500 if the giver is a grandparent or remoter relative of the bride or groom, or the gift is made by one party of the marriage to the other;
- £1,000 for anyone else.

The exemption applies to gifts made 'in consideration of' a marriage, whether before or after (though it is withdrawn if the wedding does not take place). The gifts can be made outright to the couple, or in the form of a trust to benefit the following:
- the bride and groom;
- the children of the bride and groom and their spouses (children can include adopted and stepchildren, and illegitimate children of the bride or groom);
- any future spouse of the bride and groom if they should remarry, and their children and children's spouses.

Gifts made out of income

Gifts made out of the income of the giver, taking one year with another, are exempt from capital transfer tax provided that they are made as part of normal spending. After paying for such gifts, the giver must have sufficient income left to support his normal standard of living. The first payment of a series can be tax free, provided that further payments are clearly intended.

This provision can be useful if you want to pass on money by paying the premiums on a life assurance policy written in trust for a named individual. The premiums count as transfers of value, but the proceeds of the policy on death or maturity are free of capital transfer tax. If you can show that the premiums are paid out of normal income, these transfers of value will be exempt from tax.

Example

Alec Price takes out three 25-year £10,000 with-profits endowment assurance policies on his own life, each written in trust for one of his three children. The premiums come to £40 a month each; Alec can easily pay the £120 out of his net income and thus there is no capital transfer tax due on the premiums. When the policies mature in 25 years' time, the policies will pay out around £30,000 each at current bonus rates – with no capital transfer tax due.

Small gifts

Gifts of up to £250 a year made during lifetime to any number of people are exempt from capital transfer tax. This exemption cannot be used to cover part of a larger gift (the first £250 of a £1,000 gift, for example) – to qualify for the exemption, your total gifts in the tax year to the person concerned must be not more than £250.

Gifts to support the giver's family

A gift is not taxable if it is for maintaining the following members of the giver's family:
● husband or wife;
● children or the children of the giver's husband or wife (including a stepchild, adopted child or illegitimate child), or any child not in the care of his parents – provided the children are under 18, or, if over 18, in full-time education or training;
● a dependent relative of the giver or the giver's spouse (e.g. a parent or in-law who is too ill or old to maintain himself).

The annual exemption limit

In addition to any other gifts made tax-free under the above provisions, there is a further annual exemption for gifts made in a tax year. Up to £3,000 of gifts can be made tax-free in 1984/85 under this annual exemption limit.

If you give away less than the annual exemption limit in any tax year, the shortfall can be added to the annual exemption limit for the next tax year only.

Example

On 1st December 1983, Alec Price gave £2,600 to Bill Brewer. He made further gifts in 1984 as follows:
- 6th April – £1,200 to Clive Cross;
- 7th April – £1,000 to Daniel Davies and £1,500 to Ellen Evans;
- 8th April – £3,000 to Frances Forsythe.

The annual exemption limit was £3,000 in the 1983/84 tax year, so Alec Price's £2,600 gift left £400 of this exemption unused. This £400 can be carried forward and added to the £3,000 for the 1984/85 tax year to allow £3,400 of gifts free of capital transfer tax. Thus the gifts to Clive Cross and Daniel Davies of £1,200 + £1,000 = £2,200 are free of tax. That leaves £3,400 − £2,200 = £1,200 of the exemption, and this is used up by the gift to Ellen Evans of £1,500; £300 of this gift is chargeable to tax, as is the £3,000 given to Frances Forsythe.

The nil rate band

The above exemptions allow gifts to be made free of capital transfer tax, but even if gifts are made which do not fall into these exemptions, there will not necessarily be any capital transfer tax to pay. The first slice of taxable transfers in any ten-year period is taxed at the nil rate, and transfers in any ten-year period up to the upper limit of the nil rate band are therefore tax free. The upper limit of the nil rate band for 1984/85 is £64,000 – this limit normally increases each year in line with the rate of inflation.

Careful use of the nil rate band allows considerable amounts to be given away over the longer term. If no other taxable gift has been made in the previous ten years, £64,000 can be given away tax free on top of the other exemptions. Any further gift over the following ten years which is not tax free will mean a tax liability, but at the end of that ten-year period, the £64,000 gift drops out of the cumulative total, and another £64,000 can be given away tax free.

Thus three separate gifts of £64,000 could be made at ten-yearly intervals over 21 years without paying CTT – a total of £192,000. This is in addition to the annual exemption of £3,000 (£63,000 over 21 years) – £255,000 altogether. If both husband and wife take advantage of these exemptions, the amount given away tax free over 21 years is doubled to over half a million pounds. In practice, these figures should be larger as the various limits are increased.

Gifts to children

Income from gifts made by parents to their unmarried children under the age of 18 counts as the income of the parents for income tax purposes (as does income on gifts made by anyone else under a reciprocal arrangement with the parents). Thus it makes sense for gifts of cash to your children to be invested where it will not produce a taxable income during their minority. Examples include:

- National Savings certificates and index-linked bonds – income from these is tax free;
- qualifying life assurance policies – their proceeds are tax free after ten years;
- investments designed to produce a capital gain – certain types of unit trust, government stock and objects such as port and antiques, for example.

Planning gifts

Attention has already been drawn to the possibility of a married couple giving away over half a million pounds in a 21-year period by skilful use of the annual exemption limit and the nil rate band. The key, quite clearly, is forethought and planning, so that the fullest use is made of these and other exemptions. Some additional points to bear in mind when drawing up the gifts plan are:

- making sure that you retain capital to maintain your standard of living in old age – it would be foolish to overlook your own comforts when seeking to minimise the tax you pay;
- reserving the nil rate band exemptions for larger assets such as a house or business which cannot so easily be handed over in small portions;
- if passing on a home or business on which capital transfer tax must be paid, using the annual exemption limit to provide cash for the recipient to pay the tax in instalments;
- making gifts to your husband or wife (which are tax-free), so that each of you can take advantage of the exemptions. The gifts must not be conditional on making further gifts to your intended recipients, as this may be caught by the rules against associated operations (see Chapter 2).

Chapter 5

Covenants

As the previous chapter showed, passing on money through regular gifts can greatly reduce – or even eliminate – the amount the taxman takes in capital transfer tax. Using a deed of covenant to make the regular gifts has the added advantage that the recipient may be able to claim an income tax refund from the Inland Revenue to add to the money handed over. The refund could be as much as three-sevenths of the amount handed over at present tax rates – that is, over £40 for each £100 given.

A deed of covenant is a legally binding agreement whereby one person (the *covenantor*) undertakes to make regular payments over a period of time to another person (the *covenantee*). Using a covenant to make payments to someone else effectively transfers part of your income to that person for income tax purposes, provided certain conditions are met. If the recipient's income is too low to pay tax, he or she can claim a refund of any basic rate tax the giver paid on the income transferred.

Tax relief is not available on covenant payments to the giver's own children if they are unmarried and under the age of 18. However, covenants can still be worth while for making payments to children over that age who have little or no income (students, for example).

Covenant payments can also be used to make gifts to grandchildren, godchildren or other favoured people. And there are substantial benefits in making gifts to charity by covenant.

How covenants work

Most covenants are worded so that the giver agrees to pay a fixed amount of before-tax income to the recipient ('a gross amount of £100', for example). In practice, the giver hands over the net amount – i.e. the amount after deduction of basic rate tax. If the basic rate is 30 per cent, the basic rate tax due on £100 is £30, and the giver hands over £100 − £30 = £70.

Provided there is no tax due on the recipient's income, including the gross amount of the covenant, the recipient can claim a refund of the basic rate tax deducted from the Inland Revenue (i.e. £30 in the example above). So if the giver has handed over £70, the recipient will have £100 to show for it.

To be allowed to claim these tax benefits on covenant payments the following conditions must be met:

● The covenant must be capable of lasting more than six years (three years for payments to a charity). This is why many covenants for individuals are drawn up to run for seven years (though they can end earlier – see below).

● Neither the giver nor the giver's spouse may benefit from the payments (so you can't arrange for the child to pay your gas bills).

● If the recipient is the giver's child, he or she must be aged 18 or over, or, if under 18, be married.

Even if these conditions are met, deriving the maximum tax benefit from covenants depends on two further things:

● the giver's tax position;
● the recipient's tax position.

The giver's tax position

Income tax

When the giver deducts tax at the basic rate from a gross covenant payment and hands over the net amount, he is in fact giving himself tax relief on the payment. The giver can keep the tax deducted from the payment so long as he pays at least that much basic rate tax on his income. If the giver pays less in basic rate tax on his income than the amount of tax deducted from the covenant payments, the Inland Revenue will demand the excess.

So if, for example, you covenant a gross amount of £100 a year, and deduct tax relief of £30, you can keep the £30 tax relief provided you pay at least £30 a year in basic rate tax on all your income.

Most people making covenanted payments are paying considerably more in basic rate tax than they deduct in tax relief from the covenant payments – and therefore will be able to keep the tax relief. However, there could be a problem for someone with no substantial income making covenanted payments out of savings – a person with no paid employment, for example, or a businessman trading at a loss.

Capital transfer tax

If the giver can show that the net covenanted payments come out of 'normal income', they will be ignored for capital transfer tax purposes. In practice, you can show that they come out of normal income if you can maintain your standard of living after making the payments.

Even if not out of 'normal income', net covenanted payments of up to £250 a year can be made to any number of people without affecting your capital transfer tax liability (but see previous chapter). Anything outside these amounts counts towards the year's total of gifts, and if this exceeds the annual exemption limit – £3,000 each for husband and wife for 1984/85 – there could be a tax liability.

The recipient's tax position

To be able to claim a full refund of the basic rate tax deducted from the covenant payment, the recipient's income, including the gross amount of the covenant payments, must be too low to pay tax. If the recipient's income is already high enough to pay tax, then there is no point in making payments by covenant – none of the tax the giver deducts can be claimed back. If the recipient has some income already, but not enough to pay tax, then the giver should aim to pay no more than is necessary to bring the recipient's income up to the level at which tax becomes payable. If more than this is paid by covenant, the recipient will not be able to claim back any more tax than if exactly the right amount had been paid.

Note that if the recipient is married, it is the joint tax position of husband and wife which must be considered; only if no tax is due on their joint income (including the gross amount of the covenant payments) will a refund be payable.

The maximum tax refund a single child can claim if there is no other income is £601.50 for the 1984/85 tax year on a gross covenanted payment of £2,005 (the amount of the single person's allowance for the year). For a married child, the maximum tax refund for the 1984/85 tax year would be £946.50 on a gross covenanted payment of £3,155 (the married man's allowance). The maximum would be payable only if the husband had no other income, and the wife's earnings were below the wife's earned income allowance (£2,005 for 1984/85).

Covenants for students

Unmarried children can benefit from covenanted payments from their parents only after the age of 18 – and then only if they have little or no income. So it is hardly surprising that one of the most popular uses for covenants is to make payments to that large body of non-earning over 18's: student children.

Covenants are especially useful for parents who are expected to make a contribution towards their student child's grant (as most parents are). Each £100 of parental contribution can be put into the hands of a student child by deed of covenant at a cost of just £70 to the parents. Or, if the parents can afford it, the parental contribution can be handed over in full, allowing the student child to add to it with the tax refund. The child will be able to reclaim the tax in full if the gross covenant payments plus vacation earnings, any supplementary benefit claimed and income from savings accounts come to less than the single person's tax allowance.

Amounts the child receives under a deed of covenant from a parent do not affect the amount of student grant payable unless the student counts as independent for grant purposes (he or she must be at least 25 or have been self-supporting for at least three years for this to be the case). However, payments from anyone other than a parent may reduce the amount of grant payable.

The wording below has been approved by the Inland Revenue for a deed of covenant to a student child. Copies of the wording are available from tax offices (ask for form IR47), and more substantial 'kits' are available commercially. All you need to do is complete the deed, and then date and sign it in front of a witness (who cannot be the child or any relative of yours or the child's).

Inland Revenue approved covenant for students

I [full name] of [address] covenant to pay [full name] of [address] the sum of £_____ (gross) on [day and month] in each year for the period of seven years or for the period of our joint lives or until he/she ceases to be receiving full time education at any university, college, school or other educational establishment (whichever is the shortest period) the first payment to be made on [day, month and year].

Date

Signed sealed and delivered by [signature]

In the presence of [witness's signature and address].

If you live in Scotland, the words 'sealed and delivered' can be omitted; if the deed is not in your own handwriting, 'adopted as holograph' must be written before signing.

The payments should be made to the student in three equal instalments on or just after the first day of each term. This makes it clear that the payment is intended to provide term-time maintenance, so leaving the student free to claim whatever vacation grants and benefits are available. If the third instalment is paid on 1st April, all the instalments will be in the same tax year, and the student will therefore have a full personal allowance available against subsequent earnings when higher education ceases at the end of his final summer term.

The student child should send the completed deed to his tax office, where it will be registered with the Inland Revenue's Claims Branch. You and the child will be required to sign a Certificate of Non-Reciprocity, stating that the money is not being refunded to you. Your child can claim a tax refund after each covenant payment by submitting an interim tax repayment claim to his tax office. You should ask your tax office for a supply of forms R185 (AP), and give the student child a completed copy with each payment (see Fig.1 for example). The student submits the form with the repayment claim as evidence that the covenant payment has been received.

Certificate of deduction of income tax

I certify that on paying to ......GORDON. GOUGH...

of .....FEN. FARM,. WARDLEBURY,. SUFFOLK...

the sum shown in column 2 below, I deducted the amount of income tax shown in column 3, and I further certify that this tax has been or will be paid by me either directly or by way of deduction from other income when received by me.

Signature *(see Note (a))* ......*Graham Gough*........................ Date..*2nd. April. 1985.*.

Enter here — your private address ▲

Enter here — if you are in business—
your business address ▲   FEN FARM, WARDLEBURY, SUFFOLK
or — if you are employed—
the name and address of your employer

Nature of the annual payment	Gross amount of the payment from which I have deducted the tax	Amount of income tax deducted by me *(see Note (b))*	Date on which payment made	Consecutive number of payment	*Please do not write in the spaces below*
1	2	3	4	5	*"I.R." stamp*
Annual payment under Deed of Covenant dated	£	£			
10 SEPT. 1984	500	150	1 APR. 1985	3 OF 1	
					"Duty assessed" stamp

Notes (a) This form should be signed by the person deducting the tax and responsible for accounting for it to the Revenue. Where the person concerned is deducting the tax on behalf of his employer, e.g. as secretary, cashier, etc., this should be stated.

(b) This form should not be used where income tax has not in fact been deducted from the gross amount payable.

The person receiving the payments should keep this form. It will be needed as evidence of tax deducted if a claim to relief from tax is made.

R185 (AP)   TB/8In. 52–1804/1A 551337 8/78

Fig. 1 Example of completed form R185 (AP) (Crown copyright; reproduced with the permission of The Controller of Her Majesty's Stationery Office)

Covenants for other people's children

Tax relief on covenanted payments is available on payments made to grandchildren (or any favoured child other than your own) regardless of their age. The parents should stand as bare trustees if the child is a minor, and records must be kept to demonstrate that the parents did not provide the funds. As trustees, the parents may use the money for the benefit of the children (for example, to feed, clothe or educate them), relieving themselves of the expenditure. The procedures to follow are broadly the same as for the covenants for students.

Ending a covenant

Covenants are usually drawn up to end after a set period of time (commonly seven years to comply with the over-six-years rule), or if either the giver or the recipient dies before then. The Revenue-approved covenant for students also stipulates that the covenant will end when the student ceases full-time higher education. While this is likely to be within six years, it might not be, and therefore does not contravene the over-six-years rule.

If the giver and the recipient wish to end a covenant (because it is no longer tax-effective, say, or because they wish to change the amount payable), then payments can cease by mutual consent. There must be no agreement at the outset to end a covenant early, and if the recipient does not agree to end the covenant, he can compel the giver to continue the payments. If the recipient is a minor, he may be able to insist on the payments being made even if he has signed an agreement to end the covenant.

A simple written statement signed by both the giver and recipient in the presence of a witness (who should also sign it) will suffice to end a covenant. The statement should say that the covenant originally signed on a specified date is 'hereby forthwith revoked'.

Covenants for charities

Tax relief is available at the higher rates of tax as well as the basic rate, on up to £5,000 a year of gross covenanted payments to registered charities. The covenant must be capable of lasting more than three years (instead of the six years for covenants to others).

Most charities can supply forms for drawing up covenants. Note that even if you are entitled to higher rate tax relief, you should hand over the covenanted payments after deduction of tax at the basic rate only – the higher rate tax relief will be given in your annual tax assessment by the Inland Revenue.

Chapter 6

Other gifts

All gifts are covered by the capital transfer tax rules outlined in Chapter 4 for gifts of money. However, with gifts other than money, there are two additional complications to be considered:

- the gift must be valued to determine whether there is a capital transfer tax liability, and if so, the amount;
- there may be a capital gains tax liability if anything other than sterling is given away in lifetime.

This chapter looks at both these subjects.

Capital transfer tax and gifts of assets

All gifts made in a tax year – whether of money, houses, businesses, investments, valuables or other property – must be taken into account in assessing capital transfer tax liabilities. Some gifts will be exempt under the rules outlined in Chapter 4, for example, a gift worth less than £250 if nothing else is given to that person in the tax year. And if the total value of all other gifts made in a tax year – whether of cash or anything else – comes to less than the annual exemption limit (£3,000 for 1984/85), then there is no capital transfer tax to pay.

However, the value of gifts which are not exempt is added to the running total of gifts made in the previous ten years, and if it exceeds the upper limit of the nil rate band (£64,000 in 1984/85), capital transfer tax will be payable.

Valuation of assets

The value of a gift for capital transfer tax purposes is the amount by which the giver's estate is reduced, rather than the amount by which the recipient's estate is increased. For many assets, this is quite simply the price it might reasonably be expected to fetch if sold on the open market. But if the gift is from a set or group whose collective value is greater than the sum of the individual values of the constituent parts, then its value for capital transfer tax purposes may be rather more than that it alone would fetch on the open market.

For example, a set of porcelain may well be worth more than the total value of the individual pieces. If a single piece worth £1,000 is given away, the value of the remaining incomplete set may drop by more than £1,000. It is the fall in value of the remainder that is the value of the gift of the single piece for capital transfer tax – not what the single piece would fetch if sold on the open market.

There are special rules for valuing stocks and shares; details of these are given in Chapter 7.

Loans

If money or property is lent free of charge, or at less than the commercial rate of interest or rental, there is normally no capital transfer tax to pay. However, if the loan has a fixed repayment date, or the property is lent for a specific period of time, then a gift is deemed to have been made at the time of the loan, unless the loan was made without gratuitous intent.

The value of the gift is the difference between the amount of the loan (or the market value of the property), and the present value of the right to repayment of the loan (or the return of the property) at the specified end of the loan, plus any value of the right to receive any interest or rents that are chargeable for the term. The present value of an amount due in the future can be determined from discount tables applying an appropriate rate of interest.

Capital gains tax

A gift of a chargeable asset counts as a disposal for capital gains tax purposes (see Chapter 3), and thus capital gains tax may be due on any gain that is realised by the gift. If the gift is being made to save capital transfer tax, a capital gains tax liability could wipe out some or all of the savings – as well as forcing the giver to find some money to pay the tax demand. Making gifts of assets, therefore, requires careful planning to avoid such pitfalls. The reliefs described below can be used to avoid capital gains tax – in addition to the annual exemption allowance (which allows a husband and wife to realise gains of £5,600 in 1984/85 without paying tax on them).

Note that the value of the gift for capital gains tax purposes is the value of the asset itself (not the amount by which the giver's estate is reduced, as with capital transfer tax).

Chattels

Gains on the disposal of many personal belongings may be exempt from tax if they count as chattels – tangible moveable objects such as jewellery, furniture, boats and other personal belongings. The gain is exempt if either of the following conditions applies:

- the chattel is of a wasting nature, i.e. its predictable life is not more than fifty years (for example, a caravan, a race-horse, a boat or a show dog);
- the value of the chattel is £3,000 or less at the time of disposal.

For a chattel which is not of a wasting nature but which is worth more than £3,000 at the time of disposal, capital gains tax is restricted to five-thirds of the excess of its value over £3,000 if this is less than the actual gain.

Example

Clive Cross gives away an antique worth £4,800 which he bought several years ago. The gain was £4,300 (taking indexation allowance into account). The excess of the antique's value over £3,000 is £1,800, and five-thirds of this is £3,000. Thus the chargeable gain is £3,000 since this is less than the actual gain of £4,300.

If a chattel is disposed of for less than £3,000 at a loss, the allowable loss is worked out on the assumption that it was disposed of for £3,000.

Hold-over relief

The gain realised on making a gift can be passed on to the recipient if both giver and recipient agree and are resident in the UK. The effect of this is to postpone the capital gains tax liability until the recipient disposes of the gift (and if this is also by a gift, hold-over relief may again be claimed).

Example

Frances Forsythe gives her son Philip shares worth £15,000, realising a chargeable gain of £4,800. Frances and Philip both elect for hold-over relief with the following consequences:

- Frances pays no capital gains tax at the time of the gift;
- the gain realised on the gift is passed on to Philip, who is assumed to have acquired the shares at £15,000 less the held-over gain of £4,800 – i.e. £10,200.

In calculating the value at which the recipient is deemed to have acquired the gift, allowable expenses incurred by the giver and the giver's indexation allowance can be taken into account. However, the recipient is not entitled to indexation allowance on the gift until he has owned it for 12 months.

Interaction with capital transfer tax

In general, capital gains tax paid by the giver is ignored in calculating the size of a transfer for capital transfer tax purposes (as is stamp duty). However, if capital transfer tax is payable on making a gift, this is treated as an allowable cost to the recipient if hold-over relief is claimed (though it cannot be used to create a loss – if the tax exceeds the gain realised on disposal, neither loss nor chargeable gain results).

Making tax-effective gifts

As with gifts of money, the key to avoiding capital transfer tax on gifts of assets is to take advantage of the exemptions and nil-rate band available to both husband and wife. But it is also important to bear capital gains tax in mind when making gifts of chargeable assets. Gifts should be made which fall into the exemption for chattels, which allow full use to be made of the annual exemption from capital gains tax (£5,600 for both husband and wife in 1984/85), or whose gain can be set off against other losses to reduce the tax liability to nothing.

If a capital gains tax liability seems inevitable, it can be passed on to the recipient by claiming hold-over relief. However, this should be avoided if the gain can be removed from tax in some other way (e.g. by taking advantage of the annual exemptions of both giver and receiver), since hold-over relief merely defers the tax liability, rather than eliminating it altogether.

Chapter 7

Investments

When passing on investments like stocks and shares, there are two broad choices:

- to leave the investments on death, incurring only capital transfer tax on them but at the higher rates for transfers on death;
- to give the investments away during lifetime, incurring a capital transfer tax liability at the lifetime rates, plus, possibly, a capital gains tax liability.

This chapter looks at some of the complex rules for valuing stocks and shares, and some points to be borne in mind when estate planning.

Capital transfer tax on investments

Gifts of stocks and shares are transfers of value in the same way as other gifts, and subject to the same capital transfer tax rules set out in earlier chapters.

The value of securities which are quoted on The Stock Exchange is relatively easy to determine in calculating the transfer of value involved in a gift of stocks or shares. Two prices are normally given for quoted securities: a lower selling price and a higher buying price. The value of a transfer of shares is taken to be the selling price on the day of the transfer, plus a quarter of the difference between the buying and selling price – this is known as the 'quarter-up rule'.

If quoted securities or unit trusts left on death are sold by the executors within 12 months of the death, the actual sale price may be used to value the shares if this is lower than the value established under the quarter-up rule (allowing for any change in value due to reorganisation or issue of shares). This alternative means of valuation can also be used if the quotation of the shares was suspended at the time of death, and is subsequently resumed before the sale takes place. However, only the person who is liable to pay the capital transfer tax can claim this alternative means of valuation, and the concession is withdrawn if the same investments have been bought by the executors between the time of death and two months after the sale of the investment. Gains made on sales of the same shares during this period must also be taken into account since the provisions relate to the aggregate value of such transactions.

The rules for the valuation of unquoted securities – normally shares in family businesses – are outlined in Chapter 9.

Capital gains tax

The basic rules for assessing capital gains tax liabilities on disposals of stocks and shares are the same as for any other type of asset. The value of securities listed on The Stock Exchange is calculated using the quarter-up rule described above, but the midway point between the highest and lowest prices at which sales (excluding special bargains) were recorded on the day of disposal may be used if this is lower.

However, there are problems in valuing disposals of shares which were acquired on more than one occasion. If, for example, 1,000 shares in a company are purchased at 70 pence each on one occasion, and another 1,000 at 90 pence on another occasion, selling 1,000 at 80 pence apiece could produce a gain of 10 pence a share or a loss of 10 pence a share, depending on which set of shares were sold. Before 1982, this problem was solved by pooling all shares of the same type, and assuming that they had been acquired at the average price for each share. However, the introduction of indexation allowance to compensate for gains in value due to inflation means that when any shares are sold, the date on which they were purchased and their actual purchase price must be identified – hence the following identification rules.

Identification of securities

The general rule for identifying which shares have been sold for capital gains tax purposes is that the most recently acquired shares are assumed to be sold first – the 'last in, first out' (LIFO) basis. However, if shares have been acquired on more than one occasion in the 12 months before disposing of them, it is the earliest ones acquired in that 12-month period which are assumed to be sold first – a 'first in, first out' (FIFO) basis.

Example

Bill Brewer acquired 1,000 shares in Widdecombe Enterprises PLC at 70 pence each in August 1982, and 1,000 at 90 pence each in May 1983. He sold 1,000 of the shares at 80 pence each in April 1984.

The 'last in, first out' basis of identification applies when identifying which shares Bill Brewer has sold, since there has been just one acquisition of the shares in the preceding 12 months. The 1,000 shares sold in April 1984 would be taken to be the most recently acquired shares, i.e. those bought for 90 pence each in May 1983. Thus Bill has made a loss on the sale of 10 pence a share.

If, however, Bill had sold the 1,000 shares at 80 pence each in July 1983, then the 'first in, first out' basis would apply, since there had been more than one purchase in the 12 months before the sale. The 1,000 sold at 80 pence would be taken to be the 1,000 bought at 70 pence each – making a gain of 10 pence apiece.

If shares are sold and bought back within the same Stock Exchange account, they are identified with each other: thus the old practice of 'bed and breakfasting' (selling and buying back the same shares in one Stock Exchange account to realise a gain or loss) no longer works. While bed and breakfasting can still be done by buying back the shares in the following account, this is often no longer worth while, as the following points make clear:

- the price of the shares may rise between sale and purchase;
- the benefit of indexation allowance is lost for 12 months;
- charges such as stamp duty and stockbroker's commission will have to be paid on both sale and purchase.

Shares bought before 6th April 1982

As mentioned above, if shares were bought in the same company on more than one occasion before 6th April 1982, they were pooled to produce an average purchase price. For example, if the 2,000 shares in the example above had been purchased on two occasions before 6th April 1982, then their average purchase price would be worked out as follows:

1,000 shares at 70p each	£700
1,000 shares at 90p each	£900
Total cost of 2,000 shares:	£1,600

Average cost of the 2,000 shares:
$$£1,600 \div 2,000 = 80 \text{ pence each}$$

If the value of the pool on 5th April 1982 was greater than the value on 5th April 1981, special rules are applied to purchases of shares made between these two dates which exclude them from the pool and treat them as separate assets.

Shares in the same company bought since 1982 do not go into the pool; they are kept separate, and retain their own purchase price. However, the pool can grow if there is a bonus or rights issue on the shares it contains, or a reorganisation of the company, or a pooling election (election for 6th April 1965 value to be substituted for disposals after 19th March 1968 of shares bought before 6th April 1965). For calculating indexation allowance, the additional payments are treated as incurred on the date they were actually made.

Gilt-edged stock and corporate bonds

The gain on gilt-edged securities is exempt from capital gains tax if the stock is held for more than a year. If you have acquired holdings of the same stock on two or more occasions, the rules for identifying which stock has been disposed of are the same as for shares: first to go is stock acquired in the previous 12 months, earliest acquisitions in the 12-month period first; only when all the stock purchased in the previous 12 months has been disposed of is stock bought in earlier years identified and exempted.

Qualifying corporate bonds of companies quoted on The Stock Exchange which are issued or acquired after 13th March

1984 are also exempt from capital gains tax if held more than 12 months.

Example

Frances Forsythe makes the following purchases and sales of a single gilt-edged stock:

£10,000 of stock purchased in May 1982 for £5,000;
£15,000 of stock purchased in June 1983 for £9,000;
£10,000 of stock sold in February 1984 for £7,000;
£15,000 of stock sold in July 1984 for £12,000.

The sale in February 1984 is identified with the purchase in June 1983 as it was made within 12 months. The deemed cost of £10,000 stock sold in February 1984 is therefore £6,000 (i.e. two-thirds of £9,000) – the gain of £1,000 is taxable.

The sale in July 1984 is more than 12 months after both the first purchase and the remainder of the second purchase, and the gain is therefore exempt.

Stocks and shares bought before 6th April 1965

Capital gains tax is chargeable only on gains arising since 6th April 1965 when the tax was first introduced. If you sell quoted stocks or shares bought before that date, their purchase price is taken to be either the market rate on 6th April 1965, or the original cost if higher (unless you have opted for all your gains and losses to be assessed by reference to the 6th April 1965 value only). The market rate is taken as the higher of the two following amounts:

- the price midway between the buying and selling prices quoted for 6th April 1965;
- the price midway between the highest and lowest prices that were recorded for bargains on 6th April 1965 (excluding special bargains).

Estate planning

Successful estate planning with stocks and shares means minimising both capital transfer tax and the capital gains tax due on lifetime gifts. Capital transfer tax can be minimised by the usual steps of making tax-free gifts and gifts at the nil rate of tax. It is minimising capital gains tax that will require additional attention over and above your plan to avoid capital transfer tax.

Capital gains tax on gifts can be held-over if both parties agree (see Chapter 6) – though this merely defers the liability. If at all possible, you should seek to eliminate the capital gains tax liability at the time of the gift. The following will help to achieve this:

- Making sure that you take full advantage of the annual exemption limit (which allows you to realise £5,600 of gains tax-free in 1984/85). If your chargeable gains come to less than the annual exemption limit, giving away (or selling) a suitable parcel of stocks and shares can ensure that you exactly use up the exemption.
- Using losses to reduce your taxable gains – for example, by bringing unused losses forward from earlier years, or by selling off any shares which are showing a loss and which you do not expect to see better days.
- Including in your gifts shares which are showing a loss, but which you hope will see better days – so that the gain on the whole package is reduced.
- Not giving away any gilt-edged stock acquired within the last 12 months (or parcels of a stock, some of which have been acquired in the past 12 months) if it would produce a gain.

Chapter 8

Houses and land

For many people, the most valuable of their possessions will be their home. The value of even a modest house can be enough to create a capital transfer tax liability on its own – before the value of other possessions is taken into account. Paradoxically, however, a home can be the hardest possession to bring into an estate planning scheme:

- the owner will want to continue living in it for the rest of his life (and that of his wife), which restricts the options for making lifetime gifts;
- transferring part ownership to heirs could be a recipe for family strife;
- a home is a useful asset to own if extra income is required in later life, as it can be mortgaged to raise capital for buying an annuity.

One simple solution might appear to be for the owner to give the home to the children on condition that he and his wife can live in it for the rest of their lives, thus using the provisions for making tax-free lifetime gifts and the nil rate band to reduce capital transfer tax liabilities. Sadly this strategy will not work: if the right to live in the home is retained, this constitutes a life interest in it, and that interest is added to the estate on death (at the home's then value).

However, there are ways of passing on the ownership of a home through lifetime gifts at least in part:

- the owner can give himself a lease to live in the home for a fixed number of years (rather more than he and his wife are

likely to live), with the home going to the children when the
lease ends;
- husband and wife can share the house between them
  equally as *tenants in common*, each leaving a part of the share
  to the other on death with the balance to the children – this
  retains control over the house, but reduces the size of the
  final transfer on the second death;
- creating a trust to own the house, with suitable trustees to
  decide who should live in it.

All of these possibilities require care to carry off successfully,
and professional advice is essential.

If the recipient is paying the tax on the transfer of a home, an
election may be made to pay the capital transfer tax due in ten
annual instalments, with interest at 8 per cent.

Capital gains tax on homes

A principal private residence is exempt from capital gains tax; if
the principal private residence is sold during lifetime, there is
thus no tax liability. This exemption covers the building itself,
and the garden up to one acre (more if it is required for
reasonable use of the home as a residence).

If the owner is away from home for a prolonged period, the
exemption may be lost for the period of absence. However,
provided the owner lives in the home both before and after the
absence, and has only one house eligible to be a principal
private residence, the following absences will not lose the
exemption:
- any period or periods not exceeding three years in total;
- any period of employment outside the United Kingdom
  during which all duties are performed abroad;
- any period or periods not exceeding four years during which
  work prevents the owner from living in the United
  Kingdom.

People who have to live in accommodation which is job-
related can opt for another home to be counted as their
principal private residence, no matter how long the absence
from it, provided the Inland Revenue is notified within two
years of having the second home. Accommodation counts as
job-related if it meets one of the following conditions:

- living in it is necessary to perform the duties properly;
- the job normally has accommodation provided, and living in it enables the job to be done better;
- the job involves a threat to the employee's security, and living in the accommodation is part of the security arrangements.

Second homes

There could be a capital gains tax liability if a second home (for example, a holiday home) is sold or given away during lifetime, as the exemption from capital gains tax extends only to the principal private home. However, if more than one home is owned, the owner can choose which is to count as the principal private home for capital gains tax purposes – it need not be the one on which tax relief on mortgage interest is claimed. The home which is likely to make the largest gain should therefore be made the principal private residence. The choice must be made within two years of acquiring the second home; once made, the option can be varied and backdated for up to two years.

The taxable gain is worked out in the same way as for other assets, with indexation allowance where applicable. If the home has been the principal private residence for part of the time it has been owned since 6th April 1965, or was owned before 6th April 1965, then only a proportion of the gain is taxable: the taxable gain is found by multiplying the gain by the number of months since 6th April 1965 that the home was not the principal private residence, and dividing by the total number of months the home has been owned (any period of ownership before 6th April 1945 is ignored).

Example

John Jones married in 1960, buying his house in September of that year. In June 1970, he and his wife went to live with her mother, a widow who needed looking after. Mrs Jones's mother died in October 1975 and they returned to their house. In April 1977 John Jones was transferred to the New York branch of his employer and worked there until April 1980 when he and his wife returned to England. In April 1984 the house was sold, making a gain of £67,500 (after indexation allowance).

Because the Joneses lived away from the house for a period of time, there may be capital gains tax to pay – but only on the periods during which the house was not their principal private residence since 6th April 1965:

- June 1970 to October 1975 – 65 months, 36 of which are exempt from capital gains tax under the rule which concerns any period or periods of absence not exceeding three years in total;
- April 1977 to April 1980 – 36 months, all of which are exempt from capital gains tax under the rule which concerns periods of absence because of employment outside the UK during which all duties are performed abroad.

Thus, of the 101 months of absence since 6th April 1965, 72 are exempt from capital gains tax – leaving just 29 months which count as taxable. Since the house has been owned for 282 months altogether, the taxable gain is:

$$\frac{29}{282} \times £67,500 = £6,942$$

Let property

If property is let out wholly or partly, there may be a capital gains tax liability when it is sold. If the property is a home, the taxable gain depends on the proportion of the period of ownership for which it has been let out; with a partly let home, the liability depends on the proportion of the home that is let.

However, there is a relief from capital gains tax for a home which is let out wholly or partly for living accommodation. The taxable gain is reduced by whichever of the following is the lower:

- £20,000;
- the amount of the gain which is exempt from capital gains tax.

This exemption does not cover the letting of living accommodation which is separate from the owner's home, for example, a self-contained flat with its own access to the road.

If a lodger is taken into the principal home as a member of the family, the exemption from capital gains tax is still available provided the living accommodation and meals are shared with the lodger.

Example

In the example above, if the Jones's house had been let as living accommodation between June 1970 and October 1975, then the position would be as follows:

Gain	£6,942
Less: living accommodation relief	£6,942
Taxable gain	NIL

Living accommodation relief is the lesser of the exempt gain (£47,632) or £20,000 but in the example above is restricted to the amount of the gain.

Dependent relatives

The gain on a second home occupied rent free solely by a dependent relative is exempt from capital gains tax. The exemption is available on one other home only, and extends only to the following relatives:

● a member of the owner's family or an in-law, who is unable to maintain him or herself because of old age (over 65 years for a man, 60 for a woman) or infirmity;

● the owner's mother or mother-in-law, who is divorced, widowed or living apart from her husband.

Leases

A lease which has less than 50 years to run is treated as a wasting asset (see Appendix A). The original cost of the lease plus any enhancement expenditure is written off over the remainder of the lease on a formula which depreciates the lease to nothing at the end of its life, the bulk of the depreciation falling in the later years. Leases over 50 years are not depreciated and are treated as assets in the normal way. The granting of a lease or sub-lease is regarded as a part disposal of the freehold out of which it is granted. Part of the capital sum received will be taxed as rent rather than as a capital gain.

Land

There are special rules for calculating the gain on disposals of land acquired before 6th April 1965 for capital gains tax purposes:

- the total gain and indexation allowance is based on the original purchase price;
- indexation allowance is subtracted from the total gain;
- the result is multiplied by the number of months since 6th April 1965, and divided by the total number of months of ownership to find the taxable gain (time apportionment).

However, the purchase price for working out the gain will be taken to be its value on 6th April 1965 if it is sold for more than its value based on its current use ('current use value'), or if any development has been carried out on it (unless using the actual purchase price produces a lower gain).

Selling or giving away land may involve a liability to development land tax if development value is realised on the disposal. This tax is charged at 60 per cent of development value in excess of £75,000 realised in any year ended 31st March. There are special rules to avoid a double tax liability on the gain in value on such land; the taxable gain for capital gains tax is reduced by the realised development value chargeable to development land tax.

If land or an interest in land is inherited and sold within three years of the death by the person liable for the tax, the sale proceeds may, in certain special circumstances, be taken to be the value of the legacy for capital transfer tax purposes if this is lower than its value at death.

Generally, the taxation of land and leases is hedged with anti-avoidance legislation and technical problems. No transaction involving land should be undertaken without reference to professional advisers, so that the many pitfalls are avoided.

Chapter 9

Businesses

The desire to pass on the family business to a child is a natural and powerful incentive for the businessman. Yet capital transfer tax on passing on a business could terminate its existence if the successor has to sell up to meet the liability. Happily there are reliefs for businesses which can reduce the value of business property by up to a half for the purposes of calculating the capital transfer tax liability. There are also concessions on capital gains tax which enable the owner of a business to realise tax-free gains of up to £100,000 on retirement.

Capital transfer tax on businesses

Provided certain conditions are met, the value of business property given away or passed on at death is reduced by 50 per cent for capital transfer tax, provided it is one of the following types of property:
- assets used in the business, such as goodwill, land, buildings, plant, stock, patents and so on. The value of these assets is reduced by any debts incurred in the business;
- shares or securities of a trading company which give the owner control over the company (including any shares which count as 'related property').

Business property relief is 30 per cent for the following:
- a minority shareholding in an unquoted company;
- assets owned by a member of a partnership and used in the partnership;

● assets used wholly or partly by a company over which the transferor had control.

To qualify for business property relief, the property must have been owned by the transferor for at least two years before the transfer. If the assets replaced other property, relief is still available, providing the existing assets and previous property have been owned for at least two of the last five years – relief is restricted, however, to the amount which would have been available if replacement had not occurred. Inherited property is treated as having been owned since the death occurred on which it was passed on; but if the property was inherited from a spouse, ownership is taken to date from when the spouse acquired it.

Business property relief is not normally available on the assets of a business which consists largely of dealing in securities, stocks or shares, land and buildings or making and holding of investments. Nor is it available on the assets of a company which is being wound up, other than as part of a reconstruction or amalgamation under which the business will continue. Finally, if at the time of the transfer there is a binding contract for the sale of the business, the property will not qualify for business relief – it will be regarded as a transfer of a debt due.

If the business is a farming business, then agricultural property relief will generally be available rather than business property relief – see Chapter 10.

There are provisions which permit the tax payable on the transfer of a business to be paid in ten equal yearly instalments. Interest is chargeable only if any instalment is paid late (and runs from the date the instalment was due).

Example

Oliver Johnson had included building society balances of £40,000 in his farm accounts – the amount had remained constant for many years. When he died last year, business property relief was not available on the building society balances, as it could not be demonstrated that the money was used wholly or mainly for business purposes.

Example

Arthur Butlers, a veterinary surgeon, practised from home

using part of his house exclusively as a surgery. On 26th June 1984 he gave the house to his daughter and continued the practice from his new home. Business property relief was available on the gift, for that part of his private home which was used wholly or mainly for business purposes.

Company shares

Quoted stocks and shares have the values attributed to them by the stock markets on which they traded (see Chapter 7). The valuation of unquoted shares in a family business presents special problems where a gift changes a majority shareholding into a minority one (remembering that in considering the strength of a shareholding, any related property must be taken into account). The value of the gift depends on the loss to the donor's estate, which is normally much greater if the gift involves surrendering control of the company.

For example, a gift of 10 per cent of the shares by a shareholder with a controlling interest of 55 per cent in the company would be valued at the difference between a 55 per cent holding (normally the value of the assets with a relatively small discount), and a 45 per cent holding (normally based on the price/earnings ratio with a weighting for assets).

The problem is exacerbated by the fact that values have to be agreed with the Share Valuation Division of the Inland Revenue Capital Taxes Office – and this cannot be done in advance. Indeed, it may take many years to reach agreement on a value, and uncertainty prevails in the meantime.

The tax may be mitigated if the controlling shares are sold on an arm's length basis, rather than given away. For example, the 55 per cent shareholder can give away 4 per cent of shares, with the normal valuation rules for a majority shareholding based on asset value. If the next 2 per cent is sold at arm's length, then further gifts can be made from the remaining 49 per cent holding under the normal valuation rules for a minority holding based on the price/earnings ratio. Provided the transaction for the 2 per cent controlling shareholding is carried out through accountants appointed for each party so that a market price is struck for the deal, the Inland Revenue is not likely to seek to overturn the valuation of those shares.

Capital gains tax on businesses

If a business is given away or sold, there will be a potential capital gains tax liability on the gain made. With a family business built up from scratch, the gain could be virtually the entire worth of the business, so the liability may be severe. The normal exemptions and allowances are available to reduce the tax liability, such as indexation allowance, relief for losses, the annual exemption limit and hold-over relief. However, retirement relief allows gains of up to £100,000 to be realised without tax liability if a business is disposed of – even if the owner is not retiring at the time of disposal.

Provided the owner is over the age of 60, retirement relief is available on the disposal of all or part of a business, so long as the business has been in the possession of the owner for at least one year before the disposal. With family companies, the relief is available on disposal of shares or securities so long as the following conditions are met:

● the company is a trading company;
● it is the individual's family company (i.e. he exercises at least 25 per cent of the voting rights, or 51 per cent of the voting rights are exercised by the individual and his family with not less than 5 per cent exercised by the individual);
● the individual has been a full-time working director for at least a year before the disposal.

The maximum retirement relief is £100,000 if the individual is aged 65 or over. This reduces by £20,000 for each year by which the individual's age falls below 65 (with proportionate reductions for part-years). These maxima are available only where the ownership criteria outlined above have been satisfied for ten years – the amount of relief reduces by 10 per cent for each year that the business has been owned less than ten years.

For example, the maximum available for a 63-year-old is £60,000 if he has owned the business for more than ten years; if he had owned it for five years, the relief would be 50 per cent of £60,000, i.e. £30,000.

The relief is available only on the chargeable business assets of the company – those used for the purposes of the business, including goodwill. If the company owns things which are not chargeable business assets, the relief is reduced proportionately.

Note that both husband and wife can qualify for retirement relief if each meets the above conditions.

Valuation

The value of unquoted shares for capital gains tax purposes depends upon the size of the block of shares concerned. Thus, the value of the holding of 5 per cent of a private company is primarily related to the dividend yield (a nominal value, especially if no dividends have been paid). A holding of 35 per cent in a private company is usually worth more than seven times the value of a 5 per cent holding, because the larger holding gives a certain measure of power: the value would probably be related to the earning capacity of the business with a weighting for underlying assets.

Similarly, a holding of 70 per cent is usually more than simply double the value of a 35 per cent holding because of the control that such a holding would give. In this case the asset value would be the basic determinant of the price of the block of shares.

The valuation of shares in unquoted companies is a difficult and subjective matter which can give rise to endless arguments between professional advisers and the Inland Revenue.

Passing on the business

Transferring a part of the family business during lifetime not only allows full use to be made of the capital transfer tax exemptions for lifetime gifts, it also passes on an asset which may grow in the future and pay out an income. Because of business property relief, larger gifts of business shares can be passed on using the exemptions and reliefs than with other types of asset: a £6,000 share in the family business can be given away free of capital transfer tax using the £3,000 annual exemption limit if business property relief is available at 50 per cent, for example. Transferring such slices of the family business is unlikely to produce a gain in excess of the annual exemption limit for capital gains tax (£5,600 for 1984/85).

Larger amounts can be given away free of capital transfer tax by taking advantage of the nil rate band (which allows tax-free gifts of up to £64,000 to be made every ten years). It may be possible to give such large amounts away over several years and still avoid making gains in excess of the annual exemption limit for capital gains tax – if larger gains are realised, these will be taxable unless made after the age of 60 and retirement relief can be claimed. Once over the age of 60, retirement relief can be used to make larger gifts of business assets free of gains tax.

Hold-over relief (see Chapter 6) can be particularly valuable with family businesses: an election for hold-over relief defers payment of capital gains tax until the business is finally sold. If the business remains within the family, no tax need ever be paid; if the business is sold to outsiders, cash should be available to meet tax liabilities.

Companies

Transferring slices of a business is relatively simple with a company, since blocks of shares can be given away each year in amounts which fall within the exemption limits. If both husband and wife own shares, up to twice the amounts can be handed over free of capital transfer tax since each spouse has his or her own exemptions and nil rate band; however, a couple have the same annual exemption limit for capital gains tax as an individual.

While shares can be owned by a minor, they should normally be put into trust on the minor's behalf. This is because a transfer of shares to or by a minor is voidable by the child. Partly paid-up shares should never be given to minor children, since a child is entitled to repudiate the debt.

Sole trader or partnerships

With sole traders and partnerships, the successor can be made a partner in the business, though it is unwise to make a minor child a partner – a minor is entitled to repudiate most contracts, including a partnership agreement. If the child does not work in the business, it may be sensible to make him a limited partner, thus restricting the liability of the child for the debts of the business to the capital subscribed. Although the child must then take no part in the management of the business, the child's income remains earned income provided that he carries out some non-management duties.

In general, a partnership offers flexibility in allocating shares of profit without incurring taxation liabilities. Capital gains tax and capital transfer tax liabilities can be avoided on a variation in the shares of profit, provided the changes are for valid commercial reasons (for example, if a child takes an increasing part in the management of the partnership at a time when the parent wishes to take a less active part).

An alternative method of sharing the profits of business with a minor is to make him an employee. Any wages paid for work done at weekends and in the holidays is earned income, and the child is entitled to his own personal tax allowance (£2,005 in 1984/85) to set against it (but see Chapter 3 for details of national insurance contributions).

Chapter 10

Farms and estates

When capital transfer tax was introduced, it was recognised that it could spell the end of the family farm if those inheriting farms had to sell off assets to pay the tax. Agricultural property relief was included in the new tax to mitigate its consequences for the agricultural community.

Thus, if a farmer has made no taxable gifts in the previous ten years, he can give untenanted farmland worth £134,000 to his children in one go without paying capital transfer tax – the value of the farmland is reduced by 50 per cent agricultural property relief. This amount can be tripled by making three such gifts at ten-year intervals over a 21-year period, and multiplied by six if both husband and wife share the farm.

Agricultural property relief

Agricultural property relief is available on agricultural land or pasture (and woodlands if these are ancillary to the land or pasture). Cottages, farm buildings and farmhouses are included, as is the land occupied with them as appropriate. Buildings used for the intensive rearing of livestock on a commercial basis for producing food for human consumption are also included. However, farm plant and machinery, livestock and deadstock do not qualify for agricultural property relief (though they may qualify for business property relief – see Chapter 9). To be eligible for the relief, the person passing on the land must meet one of the following conditions:

- either he must have occupied the land or property for agriculture for the two years before passing it on;
- or he must have owned the land or property for seven years before passing it on, during which it was occupied for agriculture (whether by him or another person).

The relief is also available in certain circumstances if the person passing on the land has not owned or occupied it for the requisite time.

The rate of relief

The rate of agricultural property relief is 50 per cent of the agricultural value of the property transferred, after deduction of any mortgage or secured loan. The agricultural value of the property is its value if subject to a perpetual covenant forbidding its use other than as agricultural property – with farm cottages and land with development potential, this may mean that the agricultural value is less than the market value.

The rate of agricultural property relief falls to 30 per cent if the property is let and the owner does not have the right to vacant possession within 12 months of the transfer. However, relief is available in some circumstances on a tenancy created before 10th March 1981 – see below.

With land farmed in partnership between a landowner and a working farmer, the 50 per cent rate of agricultural property relief will be available if the landowner has the right to vacant possession immediately or within 12 months. However, if the landowner can obtain vacant possession only by dissolving the partnership, he will only be able to claim the 30 per cent rate of relief, since his right to vacant possession is a condition not of the tenancy, but of the partnership agreement.

Example

In May 1984 Graham Gough gave his son Gordon land worth £130,000 he has owned and occupied for agricultural purposes for three years. The agricultural value of the land is £100,000 – and qualifies for agricultural property relief at 50 per cent. Graham has made no other gifts in the 1984/85 tax year, so is entitled to the full £3,000 annual exemption; he also has £1,000 of the 1983/84 annual exemption allowance left which can be used in 1984/85 only.

The tax liability is calculated as follows:

	£
Value transferred	130,000
Less agricultural property relief of 50 per cent on £100,000	50,000
	80,000
Less annual exemption allowance from 1984/85	3,000
	77,000
Less unused balance of annual exemption allowance from 1983/84	1,000
Net value transferred	76,000
Less nil rate band	64,000
Taxable at 15 per cent	12,000

The tax payable will be £1,800 if payable by Gordon; £2,118 if paid by Graham (under the grossing-up rules). If part of the gift was live- or deadstock, Graham could claim 50 per cent business property relief on these items, although they are excluded from agricultural property relief.

Note that if a capital gain is realised on the gift, there may also be capital gains tax to pay. For example, if the gain on the land was £10,000, and Graham had not used the capital gains tax exemption allowance for the year, tax at 30 per cent would be due on £10,000 − £5,600 = £4,400, i.e. a capital gains tax liability of £1,320. If both Graham and Gordon agree, the tax liability can be deferred by claiming hold-over relief (see Chapter 6). In certain circumstances, retirement relief may be available (see Chapter 9).

Agricultural companies

If the agricultural business is run through a company, agricultural property relief is available on gifts or legacies of shares in the company, provided all the following conditions are met *in addition to the normal conditions for claiming the relief*:

- the company's assets include agricultural property, and the value of that property forms part of the value of the shares;
- the shares gave control of the company to the donor immediately before they were passed on;
- the agricultural property was occupied by the company, or

owned by the company and occupied for agricultural purposes, *and* the shares were owned by the donor throughout the periods applying for claiming agricultural property relief. The company is treated as occupying land if at any time the land was occupied by the person who subsequently controlled the company.

The relief is given on that part of the value of the shares that can be attributed to the agricultural value of the property concerned (for valuation of shares, see Chapter 7). The rates of relief are as for non-company agricultural property.

Tenancies created before 10th March 1981

Agricultural property relief is given at 50 per cent on tenanted land which is not available for vacant possession within 12 months if the tenancy was created before 10th March 1981, and all the following conditions apply:

- the property was less than 1,000 acres on 9th March 1981, and was worth less than £250,000;
- the owner has not had the opportunity to take back the tenancy since 9th March 1981;
- the owner was wholly or partly engaged in agriculture in the UK (whether singly, in partnership, as director of a farming company or employee) or undergoing full-time education in not less than five out of the seven years up to 5th April 1980;
- the owner had occupied the property for the purposes of agriculture on 9th March 1981 and for the previous two years (or agricultural property in two of the previous five years if the property replaced other agricultural property). In certain circumstances, this condition may be met if the property was occupied by a relative on 9th March 1981.

This relief can be especially valuable, as the farmer can benefit from 'double discount' in calculating his capital transfer tax liability. The land will almost certainly have a depressed value because it is tenanted, yet relief at the full 50 per cent may be available on this depressed value.

For example, land worth £3,500 a hectare with vacant possession might be worth only £2,400 a hectare when let to a tenant. With 50 per cent agricultural property relief, the value could be reduced to £1,200 a hectare, and so an individual landowner who had made no other taxable gifts in the previous ten years could give more than 50 hectares of the land away without exceeding the nil rate band of capital transfer tax. A husband and wife sharing the land between them could each give away 50 hectares in these circumstances without paying capital transfer tax. Thus 100 hectares of land worth £350,000 could be transferred tax free in one go, and this could be repeated every ten years to take full advantage of the nil rate band.

Chapter 11

Woodlands

Owning woodlands is an excellent way of passing money on to your children, though it requires a rather longer time-scale than many of the other estate planning methods described in this book. Not only are there valuable tax concessions for gifts or legacies of woodlands, careful planning can enable woodlands either to provide a tax-free income, or to run up tax losses which can be set off against tax on other sources of income.

The tax life of a woodland mirrors the three stages in the life of a tree:

- In the initial years, planting and husbandry costs are high. The owner can elect to have the income from woodlands taxed as trading income; the costs incurred will almost certainly produce a loss which can be set off against income from other sources.

- As the tree grows and develops, little cost is incurred by the owner, and the value of the woodland with immature growing wood will be low. This is an excellent time to pass the woodland on, whether by gift or legacy, and any tax due on the transfer can be reduced or eliminated by the tax concessions for woodland.

- When the timber is ready for felling, it will at last produce an income – which can be virtually tax free if the woodland has changed occupier in the development stage.

In practice, most woodland contains trees at all three stages of growth, with planting and cropping going on as part of the husbandry of the forest. However, careful planning to keep the three stages apart can allow substantial amounts to be passed on to the next generation.

Planting and establishing woodland

Woodlands are normally taxed under Schedule B, so that income tax is assessed on one-third of the annual value of the land – a nominal value that bears little relation to the true value of the woodland. However, the occupier can elect to be taxed under Schedule D on the trading profits of forestry, in which case the expenses incurred in managing the woodland can be deducted from receipts to arrive at the taxable profit. This election should be made in the case of new woodland, when the costs of planting and caring for the saplings are likely to outweigh by far any receipts. A tax loss will be made, which can be set off against income from other sources to reduce the taxpayer's overall tax liability.

For example, if a taxpayer is paying tax at a top rate of 60 per cent, investing £1 in planting woodland taxable under Schedule D should save up to 60 pence in tax – allowing the £1 to be invested at a net cost of 40 pence. All the while, the money is building up an asset of great value in the future.

Passing the woodland on

Once an election has been made for the woodland to be taxed under Schedule D, this cannot be revoked unless the occupier of the woodland changes. Yet it is important to return to a Schedule B basis of taxation before felling begins, since otherwise the proceeds of the sale of the timber will be fully taxable under Schedule D.

Thus, even apart from estate planning, income tax considerations indicate that there should be a change of occupier between planting the timber and felling it. Happily, there are concessions which mean that passing on woodland need not produce a massive capital tax liability:

● Growing timber is exempt from capital gains tax, so that if a gift of woodland is made during lifetime, capital gains tax is payable only on the gain in value of the land (likely to be smaller than with higher quality farmland). Further, this capital gains tax liability can be reduced through the annual exemption limit by making small gifts of woodland each year. Any remaining capital gains tax liability can be rolled over to the recipient (see Chapter 6).

• Both timber and land count as business assets for capital transfer tax purposes, and business property relief is available on gifts or legacies of farmland which reduce their value by 50 per cent (provided certain conditions are met – see Chapter 10).

If woodlands which are commercially run (i.e. not just ancillary to farming) are left on death, the recipient can elect for the tax on the timber (but not on the land) to be deferred until the trees or wood are disposed of. Thus there is a choice for a person wishing to pass on woodland:

• Making the gift in lifetime – business property relief is available to reduce the capital transfer tax liability, which may be further reduced by making use of the annual exemption limit and the nil rate band. However, there may be a capital gains tax liability that can be held over but not eliminated.

• Leaving the woodland on death – avoiding a capital gains tax liability, but perhaps losing the opportunity to use annual exemptions and the nil rate band to best advantage. Business property relief can still be claimed on a subsequent transfer provided it could have been claimed at the time of death.

Tax on mature woodland

Provided the occupier of the woodland has changed since it was taxed under Schedule D, the woodland reverts to assessment under Schedule B. The income tax liability depends on the annual value of the land, and not on the profits made on felling and selling the timber on the land. In practice, the owner of woodland taxed under Schedule B can enjoy the profits of selling the timber with only a nominal Schedule B tax liability each year.

Thus, passing on mature woodland not only allows the owner to hand over valuable assets with a lower-than-normal capital transfer tax liability, it also places a virtually tax-free income in the hands of the recipient.

Example

Fergus Forsythe owns mature woodlands with an annual value of £300. He has elected for the profits from the woodland to be taxed under Schedule D and all costs incurred in maintaining the woodland to maturity have been set off against other income.

The mature woodland is due to be felled, and felling is likely to yield £20,000. However, before felling, Fergus transfers the woodland to his daughter Frances. No capital gains tax is payable, since the gain in value of the land is less than the annual exemption limit of £5,600. The gift is a chargeable transfer, but business property relief reduces the value of the transfer by 50 per cent and the amount, added to taxable gifts made in the previous ten years, is less than £64,000 and therefore taxed at the nil rate.

Under the ownership of Frances Forsythe, the woodland reverts to Schedule B taxation, based on its annual value of £300. The saving in income tax is as follows:

	If retained by Fergus £	Occupied by Frances £
Profit	20,000	20,000
Schedule D tax on profits at, say, 60%	12,000	—
Schedule B tax at 60% on one-third of annual value – £100	—	60
After-tax yield	8,000	19,940

Chapter 12

Trusts

Previous chapters have looked at the taxation of individuals who wish to pass their money on. However, there may be advantages – both from the tax point of view and administratively – in passing on money through trusts. This chapter outlines the taxation of trusts.

Trusts or settlements are legally independent bodies set up to administer money or other assets such as shares or a home on behalf of an individual (for example, your daughter) or a class of individuals (for example, your children). People putting money or other assets into a trust are known as *settlors*; the trust itself is administered by third parties known as *trustees* (the settlor may be a trustee in some circumstances).

A trust can be an administrative convenience to handle affairs on behalf on your spouse and children after your death or while you are unable to deal with them yourself. What makes trusts worth looking into when planning how to pass money on is that there may also be considerable tax benefits.

Note that there is no additional tax advantage in setting up a trust unconditionally for a single person – to look after the assets of a child who is too young to do it for himself, for example. The trustees of such a trust are known as 'bare trustees'; the tax effect of transferring property to bare trustees is exactly the same as transferring the property straight to the beneficiary.

Types of trust

From the tax point of view, trusts fall into three main groups:

- *trusts with an interest in possession* – where someone has the right to the income from the trust, or to use the property it owns (e.g. to live in a house belonging to the trust);
- *discretionary trusts* – where the trustees have discretion about what to pay out, how much to pay out and which of the possible beneficiaries should benefit;
- *accumulation and maintenance trusts* – a special type of discretionary trust designed to provide for young people up to the age of 25 (and sometimes beyond).

With all three types of trust, there may be a liability to income tax, capital gains tax and capital transfer tax.

Income tax

The trustees must pay income tax on the trust's income at a fixed rate which depends on the type of trust:

- *trusts with an interest in possession* – income tax at the basic rate only (30 per cent for the 1984/85 tax year);
- *discretionary trusts* (including accumulation and maintenance trusts) – income tax at the basic rate, plus a surcharge of 15 per cent (i.e. 45 per cent for 1984/85).

If the income is paid out to a beneficiary (as it has to be where there is an interest in possession), it is taxed as the income of the beneficiary. However, the tax paid on it by the trustees is taken into account in assessing the tax liability on it. For example, with a discretionary trust, where the income is taxed at 45 per cent, the amount of tax the beneficiary is liable for on this income, if it is paid out, is adjusted as follows:

- if he pays tax at a top rate of 45 per cent, the correct amount of tax may have already been deducted by the trustees;
- if he pays tax at less than 45 per cent, too much tax has been deducted by the trustees, and the beneficiary will be able to claim a rebate;
- if he pays tax at more than 45 per cent, the beneficiary will have to pay extra tax on the income.

In other words, if a trust pays out income to a beneficiary, the amount of tax due on it is the same as if the income had been directly received by the beneficiary.

Example

Toby Buck is beneficiary of a discretionary trust, and the trustees pay him £1,000 a year out of the trust's income. Toby pays tax on the income at the basic rate of 30 per cent only, but since the trust will have paid tax on the income at 45 per cent he is entitled to claim a rebate.

The amount of the rebate is calculated as follows:
£1,000 of income after tax at 45 per cent is worth £1,818 before tax;
Tax paid by trustees is £1,818 − £1,000 = £818;
Toby's tax liability is 30 per cent of £1,818 = £545;
Therefore Toby can claim back £818 − £545 = £273.

Capital gains tax

There is no capital gains tax to pay if the trust has nothing but money to look after. But with shares, a home, land, belongings and other assets, there are three potential liabilities:

- when the settlor gives the assets to the trust – this counts as a disposal by the settlor;
- when the trust distributes assets to a beneficiary – this counts as a disposal by the trust;
- if the trust buys and sells assets on its own account (managing a portfolio of shares or property, for example).

The settlor and capital gains tax

A gift of assets to a trust may mean a capital gains tax liability for the settlor who makes the gift. The liability is calculated in the normal way (see Appendix A). Spreading gifts to a trust over a number of years to take advantage of the annual exemption limit may help reduce the capital gains tax.

A capital gains tax bill can be deferred by claiming hold-over relief – passing the gain on to the trust. This means that when the trust disposes of the asset, the acquisition price used to work out the chargeable gain will be what the settlor paid to acquire it plus indexation allowance (with the option of 1965 value, if applicable), not the value when the trust acquired it (see Chapter 6).

The trust and capital gains tax

A distribution of assets by the trust counts as a chargeable event for capital gains tax. The chargeable gain will be based on the cost of acquiring the asset, worked out in the same way as for individuals (but if hold-over relief was claimed when the trust was given the asset, then the acquisition cost is the settlor's acquisition cost plus his indexation allowance). If the beneficiary and the trustees both agree, the tax bill can be deferred by claiming hold-over relief, so that the beneficiary pays the bill on disposing of the asset (and if the beneficiary dies still owning the asset, that gain is never taxed).

There may also be a chargeable gain if the trust buys and sells assets as part of managing its portfolio. If the trust realises a capital loss on a transaction, this can be set off against chargeable gains. If the trust's net chargeable gains for the tax year exceed the annual exemption limit for trusts (£2,800 for 1984/85), capital gains tax at 30 per cent is due on the excess.

Capital transfer tax

Gifts of money or assets to a trust count as transfers of value for capital transfer tax. The settlor making the gift may be able to make certain gifts tax free (see Chapter 4), but any other gifts are added to the giver's running total. If the total for the previous ten years including the gift exceeds the top limit of the nil rate band, capital transfer tax is due on the gift.

Example
Raymond Pyne decides to set up a trust for his sister Mary. He wishes to hand over a gross amount of £50,000 to the trust and has made taxable gifts totalling £25,000 in the past ten years. Assuming that he has already used his annual exemption allowance for the year, the capital transfer tax due on the total of £75,000 of gifts is as follows:

	£
Tax on £75,000 of transfers	
– nil on first £64,000	—
– 15% on £11,000	1,650
	1,650
Less tax payable on previous transfers	—
Tax due	1,650

Thus the trust will receive £50,000 − £1,650 = £48,350. If Raymond wishes the trust to receive the full £50,000, he will have to give a gross amount of £51,941 to leave that sum after tax.

There may also be a capital transfer tax liability if the trust gives some of its capital or assets to a beneficiary. And there is a tax liability every ten years for certain discretionary trusts. The capital transfer tax liabilities of the different types of trust are outlined below.

Trusts with an interest in possession

With this type of trust, the beneficiary (or one of the beneficiaries) is entitled to income from the trust, or the use of its property. For capital transfer tax purposes, the beneficiary is treated as owner of the assets to which the entitlement relates. For example, if you set up a trust to which you left your house on death, with a life interest in the house for your wife, she would be entitled to live in the house for the rest of her life. From a capital transfer tax point of view, your wife would be treated as owning the house.

If the interest in possession ends for any reason, this is counted as a gift of the assets by the beneficiary. So if the beneficiary dies, or loses the interest in possession on coming of age, or sells the interest in possession to someone else, this will be a transfer of the value for capital transfer tax purposes unless either of the following applies:

- the assets to which the entitlement was linked become the property of the beneficiary (for example, if the house becomes the property of the person who was previously entitled to live in it);
- the assets return to the settlor or the settlor's spouse.

The capital transfer tax bill will be based on the value of the assets to which the entitlement related (less any proceeds if the interest in possession has been sold). The amount of tax due is the amount that the beneficiary would have to pay if giving away the assets himself (though it is the trustees who pay the bill).

Note that the tax bill will be reduced (or even eliminated altogether) if the interest in possession ends within five years of an earlier tax bill on the assets involved – see Chapter 2. If the beneficiary is the surviving spouse of someone who died before 13th November 1974, no capital transfer tax is payable when the entitlement ends (because estate duty was charged when the spouse died).

Example

Jean Buck is entitled to the income for life from a trust set up by her late husband, who died in 1978; when she dies, the trust will be used for the benefit of the Bucks' children and grand-children. Because Jean has an interest in possession, the value of the trust will be added to her estate when she dies, with capital transfer tax payable at the higher rates for transfers on death. Since she is comfortably off already, she decides to give up her life interest in favour of the next generations.

The trust is worth £50,000 when she renounces her life interest, and she has made £20,000 of taxable gifts in the previous ten years, making her cumulative total £70,000. Assuming that she has already used the annual exemption allowance, the capital transfer tax due is as follows:

	£
Tax on £70,000 of transfers	
– nil on first £64,000	—
– 15% on £6,000	900
	900
Less tax payable on previous transfers	—
Tax due	£900

This £900 of tax is paid by the trustees, out of the trust's funds. If Jean dies within three years of renouncing her life interest, the tax payable will be recalculated at the higher rate applicable on death. The tax payable may be reduced if Jean renounces the life interest within five years of her husband making a gift to the trust on which capital transfer tax was paid.

Discretionary trusts

With discretionary trusts, the trustees decide whether money should be paid out or accumulated, and which of the possible beneficiaries should receive a payment. For capital transfer tax purposes, the trust is treated as an entity separate from both the settlor and the potential beneficiaries – its assets are not counted as part of the estate of any individual. Because of this, assets owned by a discretionary trust are never subject to capital transfer tax at the higher rates for transfers on death: only lifetime rates apply.

The capital transfer tax liability of a discretionary trust is calculated according to complex rules (with special rules for trusts created before 27th March 1974). The object is to treat assets held in discretionary trusts in the same way as assets owned by individuals. On the assumption that assets owned by individuals change hands about once a generation, the trust is subject to roughly one lifetime charge every 33 years, in three instalments. There is a capital transfer tax charge on the assets of the trust every ten years from the anniversary date that the settlement was created and also when a capital asset of the trust is distributed to a beneficiary. Tax is charged at a reduced rate equal to 30 per cent of the lifetime rates for gifts by individuals and the tax payable is further reduced if, at the time of the charge, an asset has not been owned by the trust for ten years, or a period of ten years has not elapsed since the last ten-year anniversary. Effectively, 2½ per cent of the tax charge accrues for each complete three-monthly period and the full charge (i.e. 30 per cent of the lifetime rates) is only payable at each ten-year anniversary on assets which have been held throughout the ten-year period.

Example

In March 1980 Gerald Deal set up a discretionary trust in favour of his children, having made no taxable transfers before that date. The trust is worth £200,000 in March 1990, and in March 1994 the trustees distribute £50,000 to a beneficiary.

The capital transfer tax charge on the tenth anniversary of creating the trust in March 1990 is calculated as follows (using the 1984/85 rates):

Tax on £200,000 at lifetime rates: £27,050
30% of this: £ 8,115

Thus the capital transfer tax due in March 1990 is £8,115.

The capital transfer tax due on the £50,000 distribution in March 1994 is based on the effective rate of tax at the last ten-year anniversary as follows:

Tax on £200,000 at last ten-year anniversary: £8,115

Tax attributable to £50,000 distribution (25% of this): £2,029

Since only 16 quarters have elapsed since the ten-year anniversary, the tax due is reduced as follows:

$$£2,029 \times 2\frac{1}{2}\% \times 16 = £812$$

In calculating the tax chargeable on trusts created since March 1974, it is necessary to have regard to any gifts made by the settlor in the ten years prior to creating the trust (but not gifts before March 1974) and also to assets in a related trust (as defined in the legislation).

The capital transfer tax computations can be complex and it is not practicable to set out the position in detail in this book. Nevertheless, it will be noted that the tax payable is relatively modest in relation to the value of the trust assets and the charge at current rates cannot exceed 9 per cent of the trust assets over a ten-year period (i.e. a maximum of 0.9 per cent p.a.).

Accumulation and maintenance trusts

There are favourable tax rules for accumulation and maintenance settlements designed to provide for children under 25 (and beyond in some cases). Gifts by the trustees to the beneficiaries are not liable to CTT, and there is no periodic charge at ten-year intervals (as for other discretionary trusts).

To qualify for this favourable treatment, the beneficiaries must have the right on or before their 25th birthday to either the capital or the income (i.e. become entitled to an interest in possession before passing 25). Up till then, the trust's income may be accumulated by the trustees, or used to maintain the beneficiaries at the trustees' discretion.

Accumulation and maintenance trusts are designed for families, and the beneficiaries should normally have a grandparent in common – if not, the trust can enjoy the favourable tax treatment for up to 25 years only. The settlor can be a trustee, as can the family's professional advisers. The trustees can, within limits, be given flexible powers – for example, to decide which beneficiary gets what proportion of the assets.

Tax planning with trusts

Trusts, and particularly accumulation and maintenance trusts, are very useful tools in many circumstances. These include:

- passing assets which are likely to increase in value in the future to the next generation;
- passing the benefit of assets to the next generation without that generation acquiring (or the settlor losing) immediate control of the assets;
- passing assets to a class of beneficiary and deferring the decision regarding the actual allocation between individuals in that class;
- holding assets for the benefit of minors or beneficiaries with other disabilities, physical or mental;
- where the beneficiary is an adult, passing income to a lower rate taxpayer.

Trusts should only be considered for a reasonable value of assets – the costs of setting up a trust can be considerable and there will be an annual administration charge for the production of accounts, tax returns and general administrative duties.

Inheritance trusts

Inheritance trusts are ready packaged trusts sold by insurance companies and investment advisers, designed to reduce the settlor's estate for capital transfer tax purposes without losing the income from the money in the trust. The trust normally has the settlor, his wife and children as potential beneficiaries. The settlor lends the trust a large sum of money interest-free and repayable on demand – this is not a transfer of value for capital transfer tax purposes. The money is invested in some sort of investment which produces little or no income, so that its value grows over the years. The loan is repaid over 20 years by cashing in 5 per cent of the investment each year – in practice this provides an income for the settlor. The amount of the loan still outstanding remains part of the settlor's estate – the rest no longer forms part of the settlor's estate, which is therefore reduced for capital transfer tax purposes.

There are variations on this theme involving loans back to the settlor, combinations of gifts and loan, and term assurance in case the settlor dies before the loan is repaid. The advantage of using a packaged inheritance trust is that the administration is taken care of by the firm marketing the scheme. However, it is important to choose a firm which can offer a satisfactory return on the investment – rates can vary considerably. A further danger with inheritance trusts is that they are somewhat artificial, and a clamp-down in a future Budget cannot be ruled out.

Chapter 13

Good causes

Although this book is primarily about leaving money to your children, many people will want to pass at least some of their worldly wealth on to various 'good causes'. This chapter looks at some of the tax incentives to encourage such gifts.

Gifts to charity

Gifts to charities are exempt from capital transfer tax, irrespective of how large they are, and whether made in lifetime or on death. There will also be no capital gains tax liability on giving to charity an asset which is showing a chargeable gain; equally, if the asset given is showing a loss, this cannot be set off against other taxable gains.

If, therefore, you wish to give some of your property to charity, the greatest tax savings will be made if you select items which would otherwise produce a chargeable gain. Items showing allowable losses which could reduce your capital gains tax liabilities on other disposals should not be given to charity – they could be sold to realise the loss and the proceeds given to charity.

Note that gifts to charities may qualify for relief from tax at your highest rate of income tax if made under a deed of covenant – see Chapter 5.

Gifts to national institutions

Gifts made to the following national institutions are exempt from capital transfer tax and capital gains tax:

- the National Gallery and National Art Collections Fund;
- the British Museum, Royal Scottish Museum, National Museum of Wales and Ulster Museum;
- the National Trust and National Trust for Scotland;
- the Friends of the National Libraries;
- the Historic Churches Preservation Trust;
- the Nature Conservancy Council;
- any library which exists primarily to serve teaching and research at a UK university;
- any local authority, government department and university or university college in the UK.

Gifts can also be tax free if given to other similar national institutions for preserving collections of scientific, historic or artistic interest for the benefit of the public which have been approved by the Treasury. Gifts to any UK museum or art gallery maintained by a local authority or university for similar purposes may also be tax free.

Gifts for the public benefit

A gift of property to a non-profit making concern for the public benefit can be exempt from capital transfer tax and capital gains tax if the Treasury agrees, and the gift is one of the following:

- land of scenic, historic or scientific interest;
- buildings of outstanding historic, architectural or aesthetic interest – together with their grounds and contents;
- property given to provide a source of income for the upkeep of such a gift within reasonable limits;
- pictures, prints, books, manuscripts, works of art, scientific collections and other things not yielding income which are of national, scientific, historic or artistic interest.

The Treasury may require undertakings restricting the use or disposal of such property as a condition of giving its consent to exemption.

Gifts of heritage property

Gifts of certain property may be given conditional exemption from capital transfer tax and capital gains tax, provided the Treasury designates it as *heritage property*. The exemption is conditional on undertakings given to the Treasury that the recipient will take reasonable steps to preserve and look after the property, and to allow reasonable public access to it. If the property is movable, the recipient must also undertake to keep it in the UK (subject to Treasury permission for temporary absence). If the property is associated with a building of historical or architectural interest, the recipient must also undertake to maintain that association.

Property which may be designated as heritage property must have been owned by the giver or the giver's spouse for at least six years before the gift, or acquired as a legacy which was itself exempt from capital transfer tax. The property which can be designated heritage property is:

- pictures, prints, books, manuscripts, works of art, scientific collections and other things not yielding income which appear to be of national, scientific, historic or artistic interest;
- land which is of outstanding scenic, historic or scientific interest;
- a building which should be preserved because of outstanding historical or architectural interest, land adjoining it which is necessary to preserve its character and amenities, and objects historically associated with it.

The exemption is withdrawn and tax is charged at the rates then in force if the undertaking given to the Treasury is materially breached, the recipient dies, or the property is sold, given away or otherwise disposed of. However, the exemption remains in force if any of the following conditions is met:

- a new undertaking is given to exempt the transfer;
- the previous undertaking is renewed;
- the property passes to one of the national institutions listed above, or is given to the Treasury to pay capital transfer tax within three years of the disposal.

Funds provided to maintain heritage land, buildings and

property associated with a building may also be exempt from capital transfer tax and capital gains tax.

Gifts to political parties

Gifts to certain political parties are fully exempt from capital transfer tax if made more than one year before death. If made on death or within a year of death, up to £100,000 of gifts is exempt. The parties for which gifts qualify for this relief are those which in the general election preceding the gift met either of the following conditions:

- had two members elected to the House of Commons; or
- had one member elected to the House of Commons and whose candidates won at least 150,000 votes altogether.

Chapter 14

Wills

Chapter 1 emphasised the importance of drawing up a will as part of estate planning. This chapter looks at what happens in the absence of a valid will, matters to be considered in drawing up a will and procedures to vary the content of the will.

The laws of intestacy

If a person dies without a will (i.e. intestate), then the estate is distributed according to the laws of intestacy. These laws may also apply if there is a will which does not cover all the subject's property – for example if a legacy is disclaimed and the will does not say what should happen in that case. The distribution rules vary according to whether the dead person leaves a spouse.

If a spouse survives

The laws of intestacy covering England and Wales entitle a surviving spouse to the following:
- the dead person's household and personal effects – for example, furniture, cars, clothing and jewellery;
- if there are no surviving children of the dead person, the first £85,000 of the estate other than the personal effects, *plus* half the remainder;
- if there are surviving children, the first £40,000 of the estate other than the personal effects, *plus* a life interest in half the remainder (which passes to the children on the spouse's death).

None of these amounts is liable for capital transfer tax, since they are transfers between husband and wife. However, tax may be due on the rest of what is left. This is divided among the children if any; if there are none, the property is divided among the parents of the dead person; if these are dead, then the property goes to the dead person's brothers and sisters (if deceased, their children). Where none of these exist, the surviving spouse takes the lot.

If there is no surviving spouse

Where there is no surviving spouse, the intestacy laws for England and Wales divide all the dead person's property equally among his nearest group of relatives. For example, if there are children, it is all divided among the children. If there are no children, it is all divided between the dead person's parents. The following is the order of priority for intestate distributions when there is no surviving spouse:

- children;
- parents;
- full brothers and sisters (and children of dead ones);
- half brothers and sisters (and children of dead ones);
- grandparents;
- uncles or aunts (and children of dead ones);
- half brothers or sisters of parents (and children of dead ones).

Where there is no relative alive in these categories, all the property goes to the Crown (or the Duchy of Lancaster or the Duchy of Cornwall, if appropriate). Second or remoter cousins have no rights.

Under an intestacy, administrators are appointed by the Court to administer the estate. Usually the surviving spouse or other relations apply to the Court for appointment, but if no close relation is available, a close friend or a professional adviser may be appointed instead. If property is left to children under the age of 18, it will be held in trust until the children reach 18 or marry. For the purposes of the laws of intestacy, illegitimate and adopted children count as children of the dead person.

Those who benefit from a distribution under the laws of intestacy may be able to redistribute the estate using a deed of family arrangement – these are covered later in this chapter.

Provision for dependants

Certain groups of people who depended on a dead person immediately before their death can apply to the Court for a share of the estate if not adequately provided for, whether or not there is a will. A former spouse who has not remarried and a common law husband or wife may be able to claim a share of the estate under the Inheritance (Provision for Family and Dependants) Act 1975 even though they enjoy no rights under the laws of intestacy.

Scotland

Under Scotland's separate legal system, the laws of intestacy entitle the spouse of a dead person to the following:

- the house provided it is worth £50,000 or less (if worth more, the spouse gets £50,000);
- furniture and furnishings up to £10,000 in value;
- if there are no surviving children of the dead person, £25,000 plus half of what is left (the other half goes to relatives);
- if there are children, £15,000 plus one-third of what is left (the other two-thirds is divided among the children).

Certain groups of people are legally entitled to a share of the estate *regardless of what the will says*. A spouse can claim a third of whatever is left apart from land and houses (half if there are no children); children can claim a third of what is left (half if there is no widow or widower). This means that in some instances a surviving spouse is better off if left intestate: he or she is then entitled to the house and contents and the first £15,000 of the rest; if there was a will, the children would have a claim on the contents and the first £15,000.

Drawing up a will

Drawing up a will is the province of the legal profession and, except in very simple cases, should be left to a solicitor. Drawing up a home-made will saves the solicitor's fee, but could cause untold and much more expensive problems when it comes to be read. Pre-printed wills can be purchased at stationers, but even these should be treated with great caution. The toast at many a legal occasion is to the people who draw up their own wills, for their handiwork can be a lucrative source of income if litigation results.

However, one should never go to see a solicitor without having first considered the content of the will – in collaboration with an accountant where professional advice is required. The solicitor will ensure that what you want to happen to your estate will so far as possible take place; it is for you and your financial advisers to decide what it is you want to happen.

Appendix B contains a model will, for illustration only, and subsequent sections of this chapter comment on its main provisions.

Revocation of existing wills

Since a will normally begins with a statement that it is 'the last will and testament of', it effectively revokes previous wills. However, any new will should expressly revoke previous ones to avoid the possibility of confusion.

A will is automatically revoked by marriage, unless it states that at the time of writing it was made in expectation of marriage with a named person (perhaps setting a time limit). On divorce, a legacy to a spouse or appointment of spouse as executor lapses, unless the will expressly says that it should stay in force.

Appointment of executors

Apart from the destination of your estate, an important reason for making a will is to appoint executors to look after your affairs after your death. It is usual to appoint two executors (though one is enough and up to four may be appointed). Someone who benefits from the will may be an executor (for example, a spouse or children). The executors can also act as trustees of any trust set up in the will, though different people may be appointed to this more long-term role.

With complicated estates, at least one of the executors should be a professional adviser such as an accountant, solicitor or bank. The executors may be able to take steps during the administration period of the estate to reduce the tax liability, and this requires professional expertise. Much the same applies for trustees, where accountants, solicitors or a bank will be able to provide a long-term service. Check the likely fees before selecting an executor or trustee.

Specific legacies

Specific bequests may be made in one of two ways:

- *free of tax*, so that the capital transfer tax is paid out of the rest of what you leave;
- *subject to tax*, so that the recipient bears the capital transfer tax.

It is easy for the tax on tax-free legacies to eat up the residue (especially if inflation has increased their value greatly since the will was drawn up). Further, the calculation of the liability can be complex especially if part of the residue is taxable and part is free of tax. On the other hand, making subject-to-tax gifts means that the recipient will suffer a tax liability the amount of which cannot be readily determined in advance, being dependent on various factors including the total value of the estate and the other provisions in the will.

With certain types of bequest, it may be particularly difficult to anticipate the value of the gift if values are prone to fluctuate – for example, stocks and shares. A free-of-tax legacy of such securities planned when prices were low could eat up much more of the residue than planned if prices escalate. This problem can be avoided by quantifying the value of the securities to be passed to the particular legatee, or by making the gift subject to tax.

Trusts

Where it is appropriate to leave money in trust, the will should also specify the general rules for the trustees (such as beneficiaries or class of beneficiaries, objects, and so on). In the model will in Appendix B, John Smith is actually leaving the bulk of his estate to his wife, but he sets up a discretionary trust to which in practice she is to be the main beneficiary in her lifetime. What he leaves to his wife is exempt from capital transfer tax, while the gift to the trust is taxable at the nil rate (and perhaps the lower rates). If he left everything to his wife, the tax bill on the total amount could be much higher on her death, as it would be taxable at higher rates of capital transfer tax.

Residuary legatee

It is normal to leave the residue of an estate to some person or persons – even if all of the estate appears to be covered by legacies. If something is left which is not covered by the will, then there is a partial intestacy with division according to the laws of intestacy.

If part of the residue is to be left to someone to whom gifts are not exempt from capital transfer tax (i.e. not to a spouse or charity), then calculating the tax liability may be fairly complex. For example, the rate of tax on legacies made free of tax depends on the total value of taxable legacies including the residue; at the same time, the amount of the residue depends on the size of the tax liability. For simplicity's sake, it is easier, where part of the residue is going to a non-exempt person, to make all specific bequests taxable, if necessary bequeathing sufficient money to cover the liability. An alternative is to leave shares of the residue to the beneficiaries (10 per cent or one-third, for example) rather than specific legacies.

Powers of executors

Where sorting out an estate is likely to be lengthy or complex, the executors and trustees may be given extra powers to enable them, for example, to take out insurance or to advance money to beneficiaries.

Other provisions

A will may also be used to express wishes as to the burial or cremation, the use of your body for medical research or transplants, the guardianship of any minor children and so on.

Where a major part of the estate is to go to a husband or wife, provision should be made to cover the possibility that both you and your spouse die at the same time (in an accident, for example). Apart from ensuring that you are not rendered intestate by such an eventuality, such *commorientes* clauses also ensure that there is not a double tax liability, when you die and when the spouse dies. With larger bequests, it is often sensible for similar reasons to specify the beneficiary survives you by a specified period (30 days or three months, for example): provided the period does not exceed six months, tax is charged on the final distribution of the bequest, not its intermediate resting place.

A will should be signed in the presence of two witnesses, who must also sign their names in the testator's and each other's presence. A beneficiary of the will (or someone whose spouse is a beneficiary) should not be a witness; since a witness may not benefit from the will, he will forfeit the bequest.

A will may be added to by means of a codicil, which itself must be properly signed and witnessed. This is often used to add a specific bequest, thus avoiding the necessity of re-writing the whole will.

Wills in Scotland

As noted earlier in this chapter, people living in Scotland are not free to dispose of their estates as they please: their spouses and children are entitled to fixed shares of the estate, and only the residue (known as the *dead's part*) can be freely disposed of.

No witnesses are necessary for a will in Scotland, though it may be attested by the signatures of two witnesses. If the will is not in the testator's handwriting, then 'adopted as holograph' should be written above the signature of the testator, and on preceding pages.

Varying a will

Anyone who benefits from a will, or who shares in an estate as a result of intestacy, may be able to redistribute what has been left – provided it is done within two years of the death, and there is no payment for the loss or gain of the bequests. This is done by 'an instrument in writing', which is usually a legally drawn up deed (sometimes referred to as a deed of family arrangement). Provided certain conditions are met, the capital transfer tax and capital gains tax bills are based on the final arrangements. However, income tax liabilities change only on the date of the new arrangements. Additional stamp duty may also be payable.

Legal advice is essential when varying a will or intestacy, even if a deed is not necessary. If any of the parties to the rearrangement is a minor or mentally incapacitated, the distribution can be varied only by application to the Court, and this will involve considerable cost and delay.

The people involved in the variation of the will (which includes the personal representatives if the amount of tax payable is increased) must all sign the instrument of variation. A written notice must be submitted to the Inland Revenue within six months of the date on the instrument, making an election for the variation to be treated as part of the will. If the variation affects the amount of capital gains tax payable, a separate election must be made to the Inland Revenue within the same time limit.

Among the uses of variation are to rewrite a will drawn up before capital transfer tax was introduced, to redistribute an estate left intestate to reduce the tax payable, to pass on assets to the next-but-one generation when they have been left to an already wealthy beneficiary, or to switch a legacy to an exempt individual where inflation has increased the size of the estate so much that a crippling tax liability will arise.

Disclaimers

A legacy can also be disclaimed by the beneficiary, provided that it is totally disclaimed (i.e. it is not possible to disclaim part of a legacy). Each gift in a will is treated as a separate legacy, so that, for example, a person who is left a house, a business and the residue may disclaim any one of these legacies. Unlike a variation of the will, a disclaimer cannot redirect the legacy: it returns to the estate, and either falls in the residue, or, if nothing is specified about the residue, it is disposed of as a partial intestacy.

A disclaimer must be drawn up by 'an instrument in writing' by the beneficiary, within two years of the death. The person disclaiming the legacy must not have received income from it or benefit from it in any way, and must not receive payment for the disclaimer. No election is required by the Inland Revenue, and both capital transfer tax and capital gains tax are charged on what happens after the disclaimer.

Although a disclaimer is less flexible about what happens to the rearranged legacy, it is simpler and may have advantages where children's interests are involved. On legacies over £30,000, a disclaimer will also save stamp duty, which may be due on a deed of variation.

Example

Ivan Morgan dies leaving an estate worth £200,000 to his wife, Jean. Jean has assets of her own worth £50,000 and is concerned that when she dies, an estate of £250,000 will be left, with a potential tax liability of £80,000.

By deed of variation, Jean switches £60,000 of Ivan's estate to a discretionary trust, in favour of her children. This gift is liable to capital transfer tax, but falls in the nil rate band so that no tax is payable. If Jean died immediately, her estate would be £190,000, on which tax of £49,100 is payable. This simple variation thus saves tax in excess of £30,000: more could be saved if Jean takes advantage of the annual exemption allowance of gifts which can be made tax free to add £3,000 a year to the trust (and the other provisions to make tax-free gifts).

Estate planning and wills

Although it may be possible to vary a will after the death of the person involved, it is much simpler if the will is correctly thought out and drawn up in the first place. Even then, it may be sensible to disclaim a legacy or vary the will, but it will be less complicated and expensive if the will is more or less right in the first place.

Lastly, it is essential to review a will regularly: changes in the tax laws, changes in your circumstances and those of your beneficiaries and the effects of inflation can all require radical changes in your will. Make the reassessment of your will part of your regular estate planning process.

Capital gains tax

Capital gains tax is a tax on gains made on disposing of a wide range of assets – whether they are sold or given away – during the owner's lifetime. The first slice of taxable gains in a tax year is exempt from tax (£5,600 for the 1984/85 tax year). Gains in excess of the annual exemption limit are taxed at 30 per cent.

This can be a serious liability in the case of a lifetime gift made to avoid capital transfer tax: unlike with a sale, no money is realised to pay the tax. It may be possible to hold over the gain so that no tax is payable immediately. There are also important exemptions and reliefs which can reduce or even eliminate any liability to capital gains tax.

Chargeable gains

Capital gains tax is chargeable on gains arising on the sale of *chargeable assets*. If a chargeable asset is given away or sold for less than it is worth to certain relatives or other connected persons (see below), capital gains tax may be chargeable on the *deemed gain* made – even though no monetary gain may have been made. Capital gains tax is due on disposal of any assets – even if outside the UK, unless the owner is domiciled outside the UK, or classified for tax purposes as not resident and not ordinarily resident in the UK.

All forms of property count as chargeable assets, unless specifically exempted. The main exemptions are:
● a principal private home;

- a home occupied rent-free by a dependent relative;
- UK government stock, certain other securities guaranteed by the Treasury and qualifying corporate bonds issued or acquired after 13th March 1984 – provided they are held for at least 12 months;
- tangible movable assets of a wasting nature (i.e. whose predictable life does not exceed 50 years) unless used in a trade and qualifying for capital allowances (see page 106);
- other tangible movable assets sold for not more than £3,000;
- private motor cars;
- life assurance policies (unless acquired for valuable consideration by other than the original owner);
- National Savings Certificates, Premium Bonds and other forms of National Savings;
- foreign currency acquired for personal expenditure.

This means that if you give away assets such as shares, land or property other than your only or main home, valuable possessions or money other than sterling, you may be liable to capital gains tax. There are, however, two important types of disposal of chargeable assets exempt from capital gains tax, which are of interest when estate planning: ·

- *Gifts between husband and wife* – provided the couple are both resident in the UK and are not separated. A couple who decide to split their possessions more equally between them (which can often make sense for minimising capital transfer tax) will pay no capital gains tax on the disposals.
- *Disposals on death* – while all assets are assumed to have been disposed of on death, any deemed gain is exempt from tax.

There is also relief from capital gains tax for those disposing of a business after the age of 60 – for more about retirement relief, see Chapter 9.

Calculating the chargeable gain

The chargeable gain is based on the *gross gain* – i.e. the monetary increase in value of the asset disposed of, allowing for certain costs. The proceeds of selling the asset (or its market value if given away) are reduced by the following costs to find the gross gain (or loss):

- the cost of acquiring it (or its market value if inherited or given);

- incidental costs of acquiring it (for example, auctioneer's charges, legal costs, stamp duty);
- any expenditure which has enhanced the value of the asset;
- the incidental costs of sale, including fees paid to value it.

If any of the costs could have been allowed as a deduction for income tax purposes, they cannot be used to reduce the gross gain for capital gains tax.

If the asset has been owned for less than a year, the gross gain is also the chargeable gain for tax purposes. If it has been owned for more than a year, the gross gain is reduced by an *indexation allowance* to arrive at the chargeable gain (see below).

Note that there are special rules for assets acquired before 6th April 1965 – see page 107.

Example

John Smith sells the holiday cottage he acquired in 1967 for £3,000 on 30th April 1984 for £23,000. The gross gain is the £23,000 less the following:

- the cost of acquiring the cottage – £3,000;
- incidental costs of acquisition (mainly legal fees) – £120;
- £1,000 of expenditure on the cottage to enhance it (general enhancements totalling £400 in the 1970s plus a garage costing £600 in 1982);
- the costs of sale (estate agent's and legal fees) – £950.

These costs total £5,070, making a gross gain of £23,000 − £5,070 = £17,930.

Indexation allowance

Indexation allowance reduces the gross gain on assets owned for more than a year to reflect the fact that all or part of the monetary gain may be caused by inflation. For this purpose, inflation is measured by the increase in the government Retail Price Index (RPI), ignoring:

- increases in the RPI during the first twelve months of ownership;
- increases in the RPI before March 1982.

The amount of indexation allowance is calculated by multiplying the acquisition cost of the asset by the following factor:

$$\frac{RD - RI}{RI}$$

where RD is the Retail Price Index for the month of disposal and RI is the Retail Price Index for March 1982, or the 12th month after the expenditure was incurred, whichever was the later.

The fraction is rounded to the nearest third decimal place.

If other allowable costs were incurred in acquiring or enhancing the asset (but not in disposing of it), indexation allowance can be claimed for each of these, provided they were incurred more than 12 months before the disposal. The allowances should be separately calculated for each cost, and added together to produce a total allowance, which is subtracted from the gross grain to produce the chargeable gain.

Example

John Smith calculates the indexation allowance which he can claim against the gross gain he made on selling his holiday cottage.

The costs on which indexation allowance is allowed are the following:
● the purchase price of £3,000 (incurred in 1967);
● acquisition costs of £120 (also incurred in 1967);
● the enhancements of £400 incurred in the 1970s;
● £600 on the addition of a garage incurred in May 1982.

No indexation allowance is given on the disposal costs of £950.

Indexation allowance covers inflationary increases since March 1982 only, so that the expenses deductible before that date may be lumped together (a total of £3,520). The RPI in March 1982 (RI) was 313.4, and in April 1984 when the cottage was sold (RD) 349.7. The indexation factor for the expenses incurred before March 1982 was therefore:

$$\frac{349.7 - 313.4}{313.4} = 0.116$$

This gives an indexation allowance for these costs of 0.116 × £3,520 = £408.

The cost of the new roof enhancement of £600 also qualifies for indexation allowance, since it was incurred more than 12 months before the cottage was sold. For this cost, RI is the RPI for the 12th month after the expenditure was incurred, i.e. the

RPI for June 1983 (334.7). The indexation factor for the garage costs is therefore:

$$\frac{349.7 - 334.7}{334.7} = 0.045$$

This gives an indexation allowance for this cost of $0.045 \times £600 = £27$.

Total indexation allowance for the gain on the holiday cottage is $£408 + £27 = £435$. This is subtracted from the gross gain of £17,930 to produce a chargeable gain of £17,495.

Losses

If the costs of acquiring and enhancing a chargeable asset exceed the proceeds of sale, then an *allowable loss* is incurred. If you have made chargeable gains in the same tax year in excess of the annual exemption limit, these may be reduced by the allowable losses (but not below the annual exemption limit).

A loss may also be created if a chargeable asset is lost, destroyed or becomes of negligible value – even if it is not disposed of. However, a loss cannot be created purely by indexation allowance: if indexation allowance exceeds the gross gain, the chargeable gain is nil. Nor can a loss be claimed where capital allowances may have been given on the expenditure.

Any unused losses may be carried forward to set against chargeable gains in subsequent tax years. Unused losses may be carried back in the year of death only to be set against chargeable gains in the three previous tax years.

Example

John Smith has made a chargeable gain of £17,495 on selling his holiday cottage in April 1984. However, his capital gains tax liability can be reduced if he can produce some losses to set against the chargeable gain. He has £1,500 of losses left over from earlier years from the sale of some shares. And he realises another £900 of losses by selling shares which are not doing too well (though he decides to buy back some of the shares a little while later in the next Stock Exchange account because he wants to keep them).

Thus John Smith has £1,500 plus £900 = £2,400 of losses to

reduce his chargeable gains. This creates a net chargeable gain of £17,495 − £2,400 = £15,095.

Annual exemption

The first slice of chargeable gains in a tax year is exempt: the limit for 1984/85 is £5,600 − this normally rises each year in line with inflation. If the annual exemption is not fully used in one year, the unused balance cannot be carried forward to another year.

A husband and wife living together are treated as a single taxpayer for capital gains tax purposes: they have only one annual exemption between them (except in the year of marriage or if the wife ceases to live with the husband by reason of death or separation). The exemption is divided between husband and wife in proportion to their chargeable gains for the year; either can choose for his or her losses to be set off against his or her own gains only, which can allow them to create a loss to carry forward for future years (even though there would be no allowable loss to carry forward if they were jointly assessed).

Example

John Smith's net chargeable gain on the sale of his holiday cottage in April 1984 is £15,095. The annual exemption limit of £5,600 for 1984/85 can be set off against this to produce a taxable gain of £9,495. He will pay tax on this at 30 per cent – a liability of £2,848.50.

Note that if all John Smith's losses had come to £13,000, this would have reduced his net taxable gain to below the annual exemption limit. In this case, just sufficient losses would have been set off against his gains to produce a net taxable gain equal to the annual exemption limit of £5,600 – i.e. £11,895. The unused balance of losses (£13,000 − £11,895 = £1,105) would be carried forward to set off against future years' gains.

Part disposals

If only part of an asset is disposed of, the gain or loss is worked out as follows:
- the total cost of the asset is apportioned to arrive at the part deductible from the proceeds of the part disposal;

- the apportionment is based on the disposal proceeds as a
  fraction of the total value of the asset at the time of sale.

Example

John Smith gave away part of his holiday cottage in April 1984
instead of selling it; the part he gives away is worth £11,000
(compared with the overall value at the time of £23,000). He
calculates the chargeable gain.

Value of gift	£11,000
Costs of disposal	£950
Net value of gift	£10,050

The costs which can be deducted when calculating the gain
total £4,120 (£3,000 purchase price, plus £120 acquisition costs,
plus £1,000 of enhancements). The proportion of this total
which can be deducted from the net value of the gift is as
follows:

$$\frac{11,000}{23,000} \times £4,120 = £1,970$$

The gross gain is £10,050 − £1,970 = £8,080
The proportion of indexation allowance which can be claimed
is:

$$\frac{11,000}{23,000} \times £435 = £208$$

Chargeable gain = £8,080 − £208 = £7,872

Wasting assets

Where an asset has a predictable useful life not exceeding 50
years, it is a wasting asset. The original cost is treated as
diminishing over the asset's life and additional expenditure is
similarly treated as diminished evenly over the remaining life of
the asset from the date expenditure was first reflected in the
asset. Only so much of the original cost and additional expenditure on this basis as remains at the date of disposal is then
deductible from the sales proceeds in computing the chargeable
gains.

Wasting assets that are also tangible and movable are completely exempt from capital gains tax (see Chapter 6).

If an asset throughout the ownership of the person making

the disposal is used solely for the purpose of a trade, profession or vocation and capital allowances have, or could have, been claimed on its cost, the full cost of allowable expenditure is deductible for capital gains tax purposes. However, no capital gains tax loss can be claimed.

Motor vehicles of the type commonly used for private passenger travel are completely exempt, whether or not eligible for capital allowances.

Connected persons

If assets are transferred between certain closely linked people, the gain or loss is based on the market value of the assets – irrespective of the actual payment. Losses created by transfers between such *connected persons* may be set off only against gains realised from transfers between the same people.

Relationships which count as connected persons are:

- for *individuals* – with a spouse (unless divorced by decree nisi), or a brother, sister, ancestor or any lineal descendant of the individual or his spouse;
- for *trustees* – with the settlor, any person connected with the settlor as an individual or a corporate body connected with the trust;
- for *partners* – with any other partner, or with a partner's spouse (except as applied to partnership assets);
- for *companies* – with any other company controlled by the same person or by anyone else connected to him; and with a trust if the company is controlled by five or fewer people (connected persons counting as one) and the shareholders include the trustees.

Assets acquired before 6th April 1965

Capital gains tax was introduced in the 1965 Budget, and the tax is therefore chargeable only on gains which are deemed to have arisen since 6th April 1965. With assets acquired before that date, the chargeable gain is worked out in the normal way (with indexation allowance if applicable), and a proportion of this gain is then deducted to cover increases in value before 6th April 1965 – the time apportionment basis. The gain which is deemed to have arisen since 6th April 1965 is worked out by multiplying the chargeable gain by the number of complete months that the asset has been owned since 6th April 1965, and dividing by the total number of complete months that it has been owned altogether. If the assets were owned on 5th April 1945, the gain is calculated on the assumption that they were acquired on that date (i.e. the maximum number of months of ownership before 6th April 1965 is 240).

As an alternative, the taxpayer can elect for the chargeable gain to be based on the market value of the asset on 6th April 1965 (the indexation allowance will then also be based on this figure). However, the election is irrevocable, and it is not generally possible to agree what the market value of the asset was in 1965 with the Inland Revenue until after the election has been made. Thus you will need to be certain that you can establish the market value before making the election if this alternative seems preferable.

Various chapters of this book deal with the special rules covering pre-April 1965 purchases of shares (Chapter 7) and development land (Chapter 8).

Example

John Smith bought a picture on 6th April 1960 for £500, and sold it on 6th December 1983 for £20,000 (net of expenses). The gain can be worked out using either:

● the cost of the picture at the time of purchase proportionately reduced to cover the period before 6th April 1965 when capital gains tax did not apply (time apportionment basis); or

● the value of the picture on 6th April 1965 (£2,000).

On the time apportionment basis, the gross gain is the sale proceeds less the cost on 6th April 1960 – i.e. £20,000 − £500 = £19,500. If indexation allowance was £44, the net gain would be £19,500 − £44 = £19,456.

Period from 6th April 1960 to 6th April 1965 = 5 years.
Period from 6th April 1965 to 6th December 1983 = 18⅔ years.
Total period of ownership = 23⅔ years.

$$\text{Chargeable gain} = \frac{18\frac{2}{3}}{23\frac{2}{3}} \times £19{,}456$$
$$= £15{,}346.$$

On the 1965 valuation basis, the gross gain is the sale

proceeds less the market value on 6th April 1965 – i.e. £20,000 − £2,000 = £18,000. If indexation allowance was £176, the chargeable gain would be £18,000 − £176 = £17,824.

It will therefore be advantageous to stick to the time apportionment basis, which produces a chargeable gain £2,478 less than the 1965 valuation basis (a tax saving of £744).

Model will

This is the last will and testament of John Smith of 37 Acacia Avenue, Hamblebury, Middlesex, and whereby I revoke all former wills and testamentary dispositions made by me.

1. I hereby appoint my son-in-law Mark Jones of 26 Victoria Gardens, Hamblebury, Middlesex, and Henry Ross, solicitor, of 6 Railway Road, Reachester, Buckinghamshire, to be the executors and trustees of this my will.

2. I give free of all tax:
   (a) My collection of Wedgwood porcelain to my son Philip Smith of 84 Cross Street, Grimblethorpe, Lancashire
   (b) My dinghy Christine to my son Andrew Smith of 86 Atlee House, High Street, Kingham, Surrey
   (c) My gold hunter watch to Mark Jones of 26 Victoria Gardens, Hamblebury, Middlesex
   (d) £5,000 to my daughter Vanessa Jones of 26 Victoria Gardens, Hamblebury, Middlesex.

3. (a) I give subject to tax £60,000 to my trustees upon trust:
   (i) From time to time during 80 years after my death to pay the whole or part of the income and capital thereof to or for the benefit of such one or more of my wife, children and their spouses and issue for the time being living in such shares if more than one and in such manner as my trustees in their absolute discretion from time to time shall decide
   (ii) From time to time during the period of 21 years from my

death as in their absolute discretion they think fit to accumulate the whole or any part of the income thereof and invest the same and the resultant income thereof as hereinafter or by law authorised for investment of trust monies
(iii) Upon the expiration of the said 80 years upon trust so far as any part of the capital and income may be in existence for such of the persons referred to in sub-clause (a)(i) hereof as are then living and who have attained the then age of majority and if more than one in equal shares absolutely.
(b) I declare it is my wish (without imposing any binding trust or obligation) that my trustees first shall regard my wife during her lifetime widowhood as the primary beneficiary in relation to both the said income and capital and that upon the death of us both my trustees shall exercise their power over the said capital in such manner as is within their said discretion and will so far as possible correspond with the provisions in my will relating to my residuary estate.

4. I give all the residue of my estate to my wife Anne of 37 Acacia Avenue, Hamblebury, Middlesex provided always that she survives me for thirty days and if she does not survive me, in equal shares to my children Andrew, Philip and Vanessa.

5. My executors and my trustees shall have the following additional powers at any time and from time to time:
(a) To pay or apply for the benefit of any beneficiary as my executors and/or my trustees think fit the whole or any part of the income from or capital of that part of my estate to which he or she is entitled or may in future be entitled provided such beneficiary is not the sole executor or trustee as the case may be
(b) To exercise the power of appropriation under Section 41 of the Administration of Estates Act 1925 without obtaining any of the consents required thereby
(c) To invest trust monies and vary and transpose investments in the same unrestricted manner as if they were the beneficial owners thereof whether or not producing income including the retention of any asset of my estate at my death and the purchase of any property for the beneficial occupation or enjoyment of any beneficiary who

would be entitled to receive or to whom or for whose benefit the trustees would have power to apply the income of such property if producing income

(d) To borrow money with or without giving security and on such terms as to interest repayment and otherwise as my executors and/or trustees may in their discretion think fit and to use it for any of the purposes of this will (including the purchase of or subscription for investments or property to be held as part of my estate) and no-one from whom they borrow money in purported exercise of this power shall be concerned to enquire as to the propriety or amount or purposes of any such borrowing

(e) To permit any beneficiary under this will who for the time being is entitled to be paid the income of any part (up to the whole) of my estate or to whom for the time being the income of any part (up to the whole) of my estate could be distributed under a discretionary trust of or power over income conferred on my executors and/or trustees to have the use or enjoyment in kind of any real or personal property which or an interest (including an interest in the proceeds of sale of such property) in which is comprised in such part of my estate upon such conditions as to payment by such beneficiary for repairs insurance rates taxes and other outgoings and expenses of maintenance or preservation as my executors and/or my trustees (as the case may be) think fit and my executors and/or my trustees (as the case may be) shall not be liable for any failure to preserve or maintain such property if a beneficiary is responsible for the same under the terms of such use or enjoyment

(f) (i)   To insure any asset in my estate on such terms as they think fit

   (ii) To pay premiums out of income or capital

   (iii) To use any insurance money received to restore the asset or if this is not possible to apply it as if they were the proceeds of the sale of the asset

(g) Whenever they have the obligation power or discretion under the provisions of this will or under the general law to pay income or capital to any infant or for his benefit to discharge that obligation or exercise that power or discretion if they so desire by paying the same to any parent or guardian of the infant or to the infant himself as they shall in their absolute discretion think fit and their respective receipts shall be a complete discharge to my executors (and/or trustees as the case may be) who shall not be concerned to see how it is used.

6. I desire that my body be cremated and desire that the cost thereof shall be paid from my estate.

7. Any trustee, being a solicitor or other person engaged in a profession or business may be so employed or act and shall be entitled to charge and be paid all professional or other charges for any business or act done by him or his firm in connection with the trusts of this my will including acts which a trustee could or should have done personally.

In witness whereof I have hereunto set my hand this 31st day of July one thousand nine hundred and eighty four

Signed by the said John Smith in our joint presence and attested by us in his presence and that of each other

Alfred Cox of 35 Acacia Avenue, Hamblebury, Middlesex

Mary Cox of 35 Acacia Avenue, Hamblebury, Middlesex

Appendix C

Domicile

It might appear that the simplest way to avoid capital transfer tax is to go abroad and make the gifts and legacies in a country where capital taxes are less onerous. Unfortunately, this is all too obvious to the Inland Revenue, which, like many other tax authorities, uses the concept of 'domicile' to decide whether a gift or legacy is liable to UK capital transfer tax – irrespective of where the gift is made. Under the stringent definition of domicility, even long-term expatriates may remain UK domiciled; they will therefore be liable for capital transfer tax on gifts made outside the UK, *even though at the time of making the gifts, they believed themselves to be outside its scope.*

Domicile is broadly the country which is your home, to which you will eventually return after however long an absence. It is quite distinct from nationality or residence, and you can have only one domicile at a time. Under UK law, you acquire the domicile of your father at the date of birth; this is known as your *domicile of origin.* To acquire a new domicile, a *domicile of choice*, is extremely difficult and requires positive evidence that you have made the new country your permanent home (for example, by making a will under the laws of the new country acquiring citizenship of the new country and taking other suitable steps). Merely buying a home in a new country or working abroad is insufficient.

The definition of domicility is stricter for capital transfer tax: you will be treated as domiciled in the UK for capital transfer tax purposes if either of the following applies to a gift or transfer of value:

114

- it is made within three years of giving up UK domicile (unless you gave up UK domicile before 10th December 1974);
- you were resident in the UK for income tax purposes for at least 17 of the 20 years before the gift or transfer of value.

The law on residence and domicile is extremely complex, and professional advice should be sought if you wish to establish your status.

Index

117